Spurgeon's Sermons
on the
Prayers of
Christ

C. H. Spurgeon Resources

Commenting and Commentaries
Day by Day with C. H. Spurgeon (compiled by Al Bryant)
The Treasury of David (edited by David Otis Fuller)
Spurgeon's Sermon Illustrations
Spurgeon's Sermon Notes
Spurgeon's Sermons on Angels
Spurgeon's Sermons on Christmas and Easter
Spurgeon's Sermons on the Cross of Christ
Spurgeon's Sermons on Family and Home
Spurgeon's Sermons on New Testament Men • Book One
Spurgeon's Sermons on New Testament Miracles
Spurgeon's Sermons on New Testament Women • Book One
Spurgeon's Sermons on Old Testament Men • Book One
Spurgeon's Sermons on Old Testament Men • Book Two
Spurgeon's Sermons on Old Testament Women • Book One
Spurgeon's Sermons on Old Testament Women • Book Two
Spurgeon's Sermons on the Parables of Christ
Spurgeon's Sermons on Great Prayers of the Bible
Spurgeon's Sermons on the Prayers of Christ
Spurgeon's Sermons on Proverbs
Spurgeon's Sermons on the Resurrection of Christ
Spurgeon's Sermons on Soulwinning
Spurgeon's Sermons on Special Days and Occasions

Spurgeon's Sermons on the
Prayers of Christ

CHARLES HADDON SPURGEON

kregel
PUBLICATIONS

Grand Rapids, MI 49501

Cover artwork: Don Ellens
Cover and book design: Alan G. Hartman

Library of Congress Cataloging-in-Publication Data
Spurgeon, C. H. (Charles Haddon), 1834–1892.
   [Sermons on the prayers of Christ]
   Spurgeon's sermons on the prayers of Christ / Charles H. Spurgeon.
      p.   cm.—(C. H. Spurgeon sermon series)
      1. Jesus Christ—Prayers—Sermons. 2. Prayer—Christianity—Sermons. 3. Sermons, English. I. Title.
II. Series: Spurgeon, C. H. (Charles Haddon),
1834–1892. C. H. Spurgeon sermon series.
BV229.S67   1997   252'.061—dc21   97-38
                                          CIP

ISBN 0-8254-3793-8

Contents

1

Christ's Prayer and Plea

Preserve me, O God: for in thee do I put my trust (Psalm 16:1).

I believe that we have in this verse a prayer of the Lord Jesus Christ. Some portions of this Psalm cannot apply to anyone but the Savior. We have the examples of Peter and Paul to warrant us in saying that in this Psalm David spoke of Jesus Christ. There is no apparent division in the Psalm, so that, as one part of it refers most distinctly to Christ, we are justified in concluding that the whole of it refers to Him and belongs to Him. But we know that whatever belongs to Christ belongs also to all His people because of their vital union with Him. So we shall treat the text, first, as *our Savior's own prayer;* then, secondly, we shall regard it also as *the prayer of the followers of the Lamb.*

Our Savior's Own Prayer

"Preserve me, O God: for in thee do I put my trust." We will divide the text at once into two parts—*the prayer itself:* "Preserve me, O God," and *the argument or plea:* "for in thee do I put my trust."

In considering these words as Christ's prayer, does it not immediately strike you as a very singular thing that Christ should pray at all? It is most certain that He was "very God of very God," that "Word" who was in the beginning with God, and who was Himself God, the great Creator "without whom was not anything made that was made." But, without in any degree taking away His glory and dignity as God, we must never forget that He was just as truly man—one of the great family of mankind—and "as the children are partakers of flesh and blood, he also himself likewise took of the same." Though He remained sinless, He "was in all points tempted like as we are." Being, therefore, man, and intending to make Himself not only the atoning sacrifice for His people but also a perfect

---

This sermon was taken from *The Metropolitan Tabernacle Pulpit* and was preached on Thursday evening, January 18, 1866.

7

example that they might imitate, it became needful that He should pray. What would a Christian be without prayer, and how could a Christ who never prayed be an example to a Christian? Yet, withstanding the fact that it was necessary, it was marvelously condescending on our Savior's part. The Son of God, with strong crying and tears making known His requests to His Father, is one of the greatest marvels in all the ages. What a wondrous stoop it was that Jesus—the unsinning Son of God, the thrice-holy One, the Anointed, the Christ—for whom prayer is to be made, continually, should Himself have prayed to His Father!

Yet, while there is much condescension in this fact, there is also much comfort in it. When I kneel in prayer, it is a great consolation to me to know that where I bow before the Lord there is the print of my Savior's knees. When my cry goes up to heaven, it goes along the road which Christ's cry once traveled. He cleared away all impediments so that now my prayer may follow in the track of His. Be comforted, Christian, if you have to pray in dark and stormy nights with the thought that your Master did the same.

> Cold mountains and the midnight air
> Witness'd the fervour of his prayer;
> The desert his temptation knew,
> His conflict and his victory too.

If you have to pray in sore agony of spirit fearing that God has forsaken you, remember that Christ has gone further even than that into the depths of anguish in prayer, for He cried in Gethsemane, "My God, my God, why hast thou forsaken me?"

In addition to being condescending and comforting, this fact of our Savior praying shows the intimate communion there is between Christ and all the members of His mystical body. It is not only we who have to pray, but He who is our Head bowed in august majesty before the throne of grace. Throughout the narratives of the four evangelists, one is struck with the many times that mention is made of Christ's prayers. At His baptism, it was while He was praying that "the heaven was opened, and the Holy Ghost descended in a bodily shape like a dove upon him, and a voice came from heaven, which said, Thou art my beloved Son; in thee I am well pleased." On another occasion, we read that "as he was praying in a certain place, when he ceased, one of his disciples said unto him, Lord, teach us to pray, as John also taught his disciples." On the mount of transfiguration, "as he prayed, the fashion of his countenance was altered, and his raiment was white and glistering." Jesus was emphatically "a man of prayer." After a long day of teaching the people and healing the sick, instead of seeking repose, He would spend the whole night in prayer to God. Or, at another time, rising up a great while before day, He would depart into a solitary place and there pray for the needed strength for the new day's duties.

Having thus noticed the fact of Christ's praying, I want now to call your attention to the particular prayer in our text. I ask you first to observe that it is addressed to God in a peculiar aspect. You do not see this in our translation, but in the Hebrew it is, "Preserve me, O El." That is one of the names of God, and the same name that the Savior used when He cried, "Eloi, Eloi, lama sabachthani? which is, being interpreted, My God, my God, why hast thou forsaken me?" (Mark 15:34). Many Christians seem to have only one name for God, but the Hebrew saints had many titles for the one living and true God. Worldlings generally talk of "The Almighty" as though His only characteristic was the omnipotent might which is displayed in great storms on the sea or terrible calamities on the land. But our Savior, whose knowledge of God was perfect, here selects a name of God peculiarly suitable to the condition in which He was when He offered this prayer. For, according to most commentators, the word "El" means "The strong One." So it is weakness crying to the Strong for strength: "Preserve me, O You who are so strong, so mighty, that You uphold all things by the word of Your power!" Others say that "El" means "The Ever-present One." This is a delightful name for God, and one that is most appropriate for a believer to use when he is in peril on land or sea, in the den of lions or in the burning fiery furnace: "O You ever-present One, preserve me!" Jehovah is indeed "a very present help in trouble" (Ps. 46:1).

I wish we could acquire a more intimate knowledge of the divine character so that, in calling upon Him in prayer, we could seek the aid of that special attribute which we need to have exercised on our behalf. What a blessed title is that of Shaddai which Bunyan uses in his *Holy War*—El Shaddai, God-all sufficient; or, as some render it, "The many-breasted God," the God with a great abundance of heart, full of mercy and grace, and supplying the needs of all His children out of His own fullness! Then take the other names or titles of God—Jehovah-Nissi, Jehovah-Shammah, Jehovah-Shalom, Jehovah-Tsidkenu, and any others that you can find—and think how much better we could pray if, instead of always saying, "O Lord!" or "O God!" we appealed to Him under some title that indicated the attribute which we desired to be exerted on our behalf.

Next notice that this is a prayer produced by an evident sense of weakness. The suppliant feels that he cannot preserve himself. We believe that the human nature of Christ was altogether free from any tendency to sin, and that it never did sin in any sense whatsoever. Yet, still, the Savior here appears not to rely upon the natural purity of His nature, but He turns away from that which might seem to us to be a good subject for reliance in order to show that He would have nothing to do with self-righteousness, just as He wishes us to have nothing to do with it. The perfect Savior prays, "Preserve me, O God." So, beloved, let us also pray this prayer ourselves. Jesus Christ, the Son of God, who was without any tendency to sin, put Himself under the shadow of the almighty wings. Then shall I wickedly and presumptuously dare to go into danger trusting to my own integrity, and relying upon my own strength of will? God forbid that you or I should ever act thus. Jesus was only weak because He had assumed our nature, yet in His weakness there was no tendency to sin. But our weakness is linked with a continual liability to evil. So, if Jesus prayed, "Preserve me, O God," with what earnestness should each one of us cry to the Lord, "Hold thou me up, and I shall be safe."

I remark, next, that this prayer in the lips of Christ appeals for a promised blessing. "What!" says someone. "Is there anywhere in God's Word a promise that Christ shall be preserved?" Oh, yes! Turn to the prophecy of Isaiah 49:7–8 and there read, "Thus saith the Lord, the Redeemer of Israel, and his Holy One, to him whom man despiseth, to him whom the nation abhorreth, to a servant of rulers, Kings shall see and arise, princes also shall worship, because of the Lord that is faithful, and the Holy One of Israel, and he shall choose thee. Thus saith the Lord, In an acceptable time have I heard thee, and in a day of salvation have I helped thee: and *I will preserve thee,* and give thee for a covenant of the people, to establish thee to cause to inherit the desolate heritages." When the Savior prayed this prayer, He could remind His Father of the promise given through Isaiah and say to Him, "Thou hast said, 'I will preserve thee,' do as thou hast said, O my Father!"

Beloved brethren and sisters in Christ, let us learn from our Savior's example to plead the promises of God when we go to Him in prayer. Praying without a promise is like going to war without a weapon. God is so gracious that He may yield to our entreaties even when He has not given a definite promise concerning what we are asking at His hands. But going to Him with one of His own promises is like going to a bank with a check: He must honor His own promise. We speak reverently, yet very confidently, upon this point. To be consistent with His own character, He must fulfill His own word which He has spoken. So, when you approach the throne of grace, search out the promise that applies to your case, and plead it with your heavenly Father, and then expect that He will do as He has said.

Observe, next, that this prayer of Christ obtained an abundant answer. You recollect the many preservations which He experienced— how He was preserved while yet a child from the envy and malice of Herod, and how again and again He was delivered from those who sought His life. He was also preserved many times from falling into the snares set for Him by scribes and Pharisees and others who sought to entrap Him in His talk. How wisely He answered the lawyer who came to Him tempting Him, and those who sought to catch Him over the matter of paying tribute to Caesar! He was never taken as a bird ensnared by the fowler. He was always preserved in every emergency. He was like a physician in a hospital full of lepers, yet he was always preserved from the contagion.

Then, to close this part of the subject, notice that this prayer most deeply concerns the whole company of believers in Christ, for it strikes me that, when our Savior prayed to His Father, "Preserve me," he was thinking of the whole of His mystical body, and pleading for all who were vitally united to Him. You remember how in His great intercessory supplication He pleaded for His disciples, "Holy Father, keep through thine own name those whom thou hast given me, that they may be one, as we are" (John 17:11). This is the same prayer as "Preserve me" if we understand the "me" to include all who are one with Christ. We also are included in that supplication, for He further said, "Neither pray I for these alone, but for them also which shall believe on me through their word; that they all may be one; as thou, Father, art in me, and I in thee, that they also may be one in us: that the world may believe that thou hast sent me" (John 17:20–21). Yes, dear friend, though you may seem to yourself to be the meanest of the Lord's people, even though you are in your own apprehension but as His feet that glow in the furnace of affliction, even you are among those whom Christ entreated His Father to keep. You may rest assured that He will certainly do so. Christ will never lose one of the members of His mystical body. If He could do so, His body would be imperfect and incomplete, but that it never can be. Paul tells us that Christ's church "is his body, the fulness of him that filleth all in all" (Eph. 1:23), so that, if He were left without His fullness, He would have suffered an irreparable loss. That can never be the case, so this prayer will be answered concerning the whole body of believers in Jesus who shall be presented "faultless before the presence of his glory with exceeding joy" (Jude 24), blessed be His holy name!

Let us now turn to *the plea which Christ urged in support of His prayer:* "Preserve me, O God: for in thee do I put my trust." Did Christ put His trust in His Father? We scarcely need to ask the question, and we know at once what the answer must be. In the matter of faith, as in everything else, He is a perfect example to His people, and we cannot imagine a Christian without faith. Faith is the very life of a true believer in Jesus. Indeed, without faith he is not a believer, so Christ was his model in this respect as well as in every other.

The words "in thee do I put my trust" may be translated, "in You do I shelter." There is in them an allusion to running under something for shelter. In fact, the best figure I can use to give you the meaning of this sentence is that of the chickens running under the wings of the hen for shelter. Just so do we hide ourselves under the overshadowing wings of the Eternal. As a man, Christ used this plea with God that He was sheltering from all evil under the divine wings of power, wisdom, goodness, and truth. This is an accurate interpretation of the passage, and there are many instances recorded in Scripture in which Christ really did this. Take, for instance, that remarkable declaration in Psalm 22:9: "Thou didst make me hope when I was upon my mother's breasts," as though very early in life, probably far earlier than any of us were brought to know the Lord, Jesus Christ was exercising hope in the Most High. Then again in the fiftieth chapter of the prophecy of Isaiah we have these words which must refer to the Lord Jesus Christ, "I gave my back to the smiters, and my cheeks to the them that plucked off the hair: I hid not my face from shame and spitting" (v. 6). That verse is immediately followed by this one, "For the Lord GOD will help me; therefore shall I not be confounded: therefore have I set my face like a flint, and I know that I shall not be ashamed" (v. 7). These words were peculiarly appropriate from the lips of Christ, yet each one of His followers may also say, "The Lord God will help me."

Even in his last agonies Christ uttered words which plainly prove that He had put His trust in God, "Father, into thy hands I commend my spirit" (Luke 23:46). There is more faith in that final commendation of His soul to His Father than some of you might imagine, for it takes great faith to be able to speak thus in the circumstances in which Christ was then placed. Not only was He suffering the terrible pangs that were inseparable from death by crucifixion, but He had to bear the still greater grief that was His portion when His Father's face was withdrawn from Him because He was in the place of sinners and, therefore, had to endure the separation from God which was their due. Job said, "Though he slay me, yet will I trust in him" (13:15), and this was what Jesus actually did. What wondrous faith it was that trusted in God even when He said, "Awake, O sword, against my shepherd, and against the man that is my fellow, saith the LORD of hosts" (Zech. 13:7)! Yet even then Jesus turned to His Father and said, "'Father, into thy hands I commend my spirit;' I commit Myself into the hand that wields the sword of infallible justice, into the hand that has crushed Me and broken Me in pieces."

Talk of faith, did you ever hear of such sublime confidence as that having been displayed by anyone else? When a martyr has to lay down his life for the truth, his faith is sustained by the comforting presence of

God. He believes in the God who is smiling upon him even while he is in the midst of the fire. But Christ on the cross trusted in the God who had forsaken Him. O beloved, imitate this faith so far as it is possible in your case! What a glorious height of confidence Jesus reached. Oh, that we may have grace to follow where He has so blessedly led the way!

I want you carefully to notice the argument that is contained in Christ's plea: "Preserve me, O God: for in thee do I put my trust." Christ, as God, had felt the power of that plea, so He knew that His Father would also feel the power of it. You remember that Jesus said to the woman of Canaan, "O woman, great is thy faith: be it unto thee even as thou wilt" (Matt. 15:28). Her faith prevailed with Him, and He felt that His faith would prevail with His Father. So that, when He said, "In thee do I put my trust," He knew that He would obtain the preservation for which He pleaded. Jesus never forgot that the rule of the kingdom is, "According to your faith be it unto you" (Matt. 9:29). He knew that we must "ask in faith, nothing wavering. For he that wavereth is like a wave of the sea driven with the wind and tossed. For let not that man think that he shall receive any thing of the Lord" (James 1:6–7). So Jesus came to His Father with this plea, "I do trust in You. I have absolute confidence in You, therefore I pray You to preserve Me."

My dear brother or sister in Christ, can you say the same? Can you look up to God and say, "In thee do I put my trust"? If so, you may use it as Christ used it in pleading with His Father. Perhaps you have gazed upon a weapon that has been wielded by some great warrior. If you had that weapon in your hand and were going forth to fight, you would feel, "I must not be a coward while I am grasping a brave man's sword, but I must play the man with it as he did." Well, you have in your grasp the very weapon which Christ used when He gained the victory. You can go before God with the very same argument that Christ used with His Father, and He will hear your plea even as He heard Christ's: "Preserve me, O God: for in thee do I put my trust."

The Prayer of Christ's Followers

I had intended, in the second place, to speak of my text as the prayer of Christ's followers. But, instead of preaching upon it as I would have done had time permitted, I will merely give you a few notes upon it. Then you can preach the second sermon yourselves by practicing it as you go your several ways to your homes.

First, *what does this prayer mean to a believer?* It means that you put yourself and all belonging to you under divine protection. Before you close your eyes, pray this prayer: "'Preserve me, O God!' Preserve my body, my family, my house, from fire, from famine, from hurt or harm of every kind." Specially present the prayer in a spiritual sense:

"Preserve me from the world. Let me not be carried away with its excitements. Suffer me not to bow before its blandishments nor to fear its frowns. Preserve me from the Devil. Let him not tempt me above what I am able to bear. Preserve me from myself. Keep me from growing envious, selfish, high-minded, proud, slothful. Preserve me from those evils into which I see others run, and preserve me from those evils into which I am myself most apt to run; keep me from evils known and from evils unknown. 'Cleanse thou me from secret faults. Keep back thy servant also from presumptuous sins; let them not have dominion over me.'"

This is a prayer which is more comprehensive in the original than it is in our version. It may be translated, "Save me," and this is a prayer that is suitable for many here. Those of you who have never prayed before can begin with this prayer, "Save me, O strong One! It will indeed need a strong One to save me, for I am so far gone that nothing but omnipotence can save me." It may also be rendered, "Keep me," or "Guard me." It is the word which we should use in speaking of the bodyguard of a king or of shepherds protecting their flocks. It is a prayer which you may keep on using from the time you begin to know the Lord until you get to heaven. Then you will only need to alter Jude's Doxology very slightly and to say, "Unto him who has kept us from falling, and presents us faultless before the presence of his glory with exceeding joy, to the only wise God our Savior, be glory and majesty, dominion and power, both now and ever. Amen."

Next, *when is this prayer suitable?* Well, it is suitable at this moment. You do not know what dangers you will meet with before you go to your bed tonight. Take special care when you come to what you consider the safe parts of the road, for you will probably be most in danger when you think you are in no danger at all. It is often a greater peril not to be tempted than to be tempted. This prayer is suitable to some of you who are going into new situations where you will have new responsibilities, new duties, and probably new trials and difficulties. In the old days of superstition, people were foolish enough to wear charms of various kinds to guard them from evil. But such a prayer as this is better than all their charms. If your pathway should be through the enchanted fields or even through the valley of death-shade, you need not be afraid but may march boldly on with this prayer on your lips, "Preserve me, O God: for in thee do I put my trust."

Then, *in what spirit ought this prayer to be offered?* It should be offered in a spirit of deep humility. Do not pray, "Preserve me, O God," as though you felt that you were a very precious person. It is true that God regards you as one of His jewels if you are a believer in Jesus, but you are not to regard yourself as a jewel. Think of yourself as a brand plucked from the burning, and then you will pray with due humility.

Pray as a poor feeble creature who must be destroyed unless God shall preserve you. Pray as if you were a sheep that had been shorn and that needed to have the wind tempered to it. Pray as a drowning man might pray, "Preserve me, O God." Pray as sinking Peter prayed, "Lord, save me," for so you shall be preserved even as He was.

With what motive ought you to pray this prayer? Pray it specially out of hatred to sin. Whenever you think of sin, the best thing you can do is to pray, "Preserve me, O God." Whenever you hear or read of others doing wrong, do not begin to plume yourself upon your own excellence, but cry at once, "Preserve me, O God, or it may be that I shall sin even as those others have done." If this night you are a Christian, the praise for this is not to be given to yourself, but to the Lord who has made you to differ from others. You are only what His grace has made you, so show how highly you value that grace by asking for more and more of it.

This must suffice concerning the prayer of the text, for I must, in closing, remind you of the plea and ask if each one here is able to use it: "Preserve me, O God: *for in thee do I put my trust.*" O you, my friend, urge this plea with God tonight. Perhaps you say that you could do so years ago, then why not put your trust in the Lord now? It is present faith that you need in your present perils, and you cannot pray acceptably without faith, "for he that cometh to God must believe that he is, and that he is a rewarder of them that diligently seek him." You know what it is to trust a friend, and perhaps to be deceived. But do you know what it is to trust in God and not be deceived? Are you trusting for salvation only to Christ? Do you sing—

> Thou, O Christ, art all I want,
> More than all in thee I find?

Is this your plea continually? Are you always trusting in God, in the dark as well as in the light? Many a man thinks he is strong until he begins to put forth his strength, and then he finds that it is utter weakness. There are many who fancy they are full of faith until they try to exercise it, and then they realize how little they have. They are fine soldiers when there is no fighting, and splendid sailors as long as they are on dry land. But such faith as that is of little service when some great emergency arises. The faith we need is that firm confidence which sings—

> His love in time past forbids me to think
> He'll leave me at last in trouble to sink;
> Each sweet Ebenezer I have in review
> Confirms his good pleasure to help me quite through.

If that is the kind of faith you have, you need not fear to pray, "Preserve me, O God," for He will be as a wall of fire around you to guard you from all evil. Though you are now in the midst of those who would drag you down to their level if they could or turn you aside from the paths of righteousness, the Lord in whom you have put your trust will never leave you nor forsake you. Instead He will bring you in His own good time to that blessed place of which He has told you in His Word. There—

> Far from a world of grief and sin,
> With God eternally shut in—

you shall be preserved from all evil forever, and faith shall be blessedly exchanged for sight. God grant that every one of us may be able to pray the prayer of our text and to use the plea, "Preserve me, O God: for in thee have I put my trust," for Jesus' sake! Amen.

2

Our Lord's Solemn Inquiry

Eli, Eli, lama sabachthani? that is to say, My God, my God, why hast thou forsaken me? (Matthew 27:46).

If any one of us, lovers of the Lord Jesus Christ, had been anywhere near the cross when He uttered those words, I am sure our hearts would have burst with anguish. One thing is certain, we would have heard the tones of that dying cry as long as ever we lived. There is no doubt that at certain times they would come to us again, ringing shrill and clear through the thick darkness. We would remember just how they were uttered, and the emphasis where it was placed. I have no doubt we would turn that text over and over and over in our minds. But there is one thing, I think, we could never have done if we had heard it—therefore, I am not going to do it—we would never preach from it. It would have been too painful a recollection for us ever to have used it as a text. No; we would have said, "It is enough to hear it." Fully understand it, who can? And to expound it, since some measure of understanding might be necessary to the exposition—that surely would be a futile attempt. We would have laid that by. We would have put those words away as too sacred, too solemn, except for silent reflection and quiet, reverent adoration. I felt when I read these words again, as I have often read them, that they seemed to say to me, "You cannot preach from us." On the other hand, I felt as Moses did when he put off his shoes from his feet in the presence of the burning bush because the place whereon he stood was holy ground.

Beloved, there is another reason why we should not venture to preach from this text, namely, that it is probably an expression out of the lowest depths of our Savior's sufferings. With Him into the seas of

---

This sermon was taken from *The Metropolitan Tabernacle Pulpit* and was preached on Sunday evening, April 7, 1872.

17

grief we can descend some part of the way, but when He comes where all God's waves and billows go over Him, we cannot go there. We may, indeed, drink of His cup and be baptized with His baptism, but never to the full extent. Therefore, where our fellowship with Christ cannot conduct us to the full, though it may in a measure, we shall not venture. We shall not venture beyond where our fellowship with Him would lead us aright, lest we blunder by speculation and "darken counsel by words without knowledge." Moreover, it comes forcibly upon my mind that though every word here is emphatic, we would be pretty sure to put the emphasis somewhere or other too little. I do not suppose we would be likely to put it anywhere too much.

It has been well said that every word in this memorable cry deserves to have an emphasis laid upon it. If you read it, "My God, My God, why have *You* forsaken Me? I marvel not that My disciples should, but why have You gone, My Father, God? Why could *You* leave Me?" There is a wondrous meaning there. Then take it thus, "My God, My God, why have You *forsaken* Me? I know why You have smitten Me. I can understand why You do chasten Me. But why have You *forsaken* Me? Will You allow Me no ray of love from the brightness of Your eyes—no sense of Your presence whatsoever?" This was the wormwood and the gall of all the Savior's bitter cup. Then God forsook Him in His direst need. Or if you take it thus, "My God, My God, why have You forsaken *Me?*" there comes another meaning. "*Me,* Your well beloved, Your eternal well beloved, Your innocent, Your harmless, Your afflicted Son— why have You forsaken *Me?*" Then, indeed, it is a marvel of marvels not that God would forsake His saints, or appear to do so, or that He would forsake sinners utterly, but that He would forsake His only Son. Then, again, we might with great propriety throw the whole force of the verse upon the particle of interrogation, "Why." "My God, My God, *why,* ah! why have You forsaken Me? What is Your reason? What is Your motive? What compels You to this, Lord of love? The sun is eclipsed, but why is the Son of Your love eclipsed? You have taken away the lives of men for sin, but why take away Your love, which is My life, from Me who has no sin? Why and wherefore do You act thus?"

Now, as I have said, every word requires more emphasis than I can throw into it, and some part of the text would be quite sure to be left and not dealt with as it should be. Therefore, we will not think of preaching upon it, but instead thereof we will sit down and commune with it.

You must know that the words of our text are not only the language of Christ, but they are the language of David. You who are acquainted with the Psalms know that the Psalm 22 begins with just these words, so that David said what Jesus said. I gather from this that many a child of God has had to say precisely what the Lord Jesus, the first-born of the family, uttered upon the cross. Now as God's children are brought into the same circumstances as Christ, and Christ is considered the exemplar, my object tonight will be simply this—not to expound the words, but to say to believers who come into a similar plight, Do as Jesus did. If you come into His condition, lift up your hearts to God that you may act as He did in that condition. So we shall make the Savior now not a study for our learning, but an example for reproduction. The first out of these points in which, I think, we should imitate Him is this:

Under Desertion of Soul, the Lord Jesus Still Turns to God

At that time when He uttered these words, God had left Him to His enemies. No angel appeared to interpose and destroy the power of Roman or Jew. He seemed utterly given up. The people might mock at Him and might put Him to what pain they pleased, at the same time a sense of God's love to Him as man was taken from Him. The comfortable presence of God that had all His life long sustained Him began to withdraw from Him in the garden, and appeared to be quite gone when He was just in the article of death upon the cross. Meanwhile the waves of God's wrath on account of sin began to break over His spirit, and He was in the condition of a soul deserted by God. Now sometimes believers come into the same condition, not to the same extent, but in a measure. Yesterday they were full of joy, for the love of God was shed abroad in their hearts, but today that sense of love is gone. They droop; they feel heavy. Now the temptation will be at such times for them to sit down and look into their own hearts. If they do, they will grow more wretched every moment until they will come well nigh to despair, for there is no comfort to be found within when there is no light from above. Our signs and tokens within are like sundials. We can tell what time it is by the sundial when the sun shines, but if it does not, what is the use of the sundial? And so marks of evidence may help us when God's love is shed abroad in the soul, but when that is gone, marks of evidence stand us in very little stead.

Now observe our Lord. He is deserted of God, but instead of looking in and saying, "My soul, why are you this? Why are you that? Why are you cast down? Why do you mourn?" He looks straight away from that dried-up well that is within to those eternal waters that never can be stayed and which are always full of refreshment. He cries, "My God." He knows which way to look. I say to every Christian here, it is a temptation of the Devil when you are desponding and are not enjoying your relationship with Christ, as you did, to begin peering and searching about in the dunghill of your own corruptions, and stirring over all that you are feeling, all you ought to feel, and all you do not feel, and all that. Instead of that, look from within, look above, look to your God again, for the light will come there.

And you will notice that *our Lord did not at this time look to any of His friends.* In the beginning of His sufferings He appeared to seek consolation from His disciples, but He found them sleeping for sorrow. Therefore, on this occasion He did not look to them in any measure. He had lost the light of God's countenance, but He does not look down in the darkness and say, "John, dear faithful John, are you there? Have you not a word for Him whose bosom was a pillow for your head? Mother Mary, are you there? Can you not say one soft word to your dying Son to let Him know there is still a heart that does not forget Him?" No, beloved; our Lord did not look to the creature. Man as He was, and we must regard him as such in uttering this cry, yet He does not look to friend or brother, helper or human arm. But though God be angry, as it were, yet He cries, "My God." Oh! it is the only cry that befits a believer's lips. Even if God seems to forsake you, keep on crying to Him. Do not begin to look in a pet and a jealous humor to creatures, but still look to your God. Depend upon it, He will come to you sooner or later. He cannot fail you. He must help you. Like a child if its mother strikes it, still if the child be in pain it cries for its mother. It knows her love. It knows its deep need of her and that she alone can supply its need.

Oh! beloved, do the same. Is there one in this house who has lately lost his comforts and Satan has said, "Don't pray"? Beloved, pray more than ever you did. If the Devil says, "Why, God is angry. What is the use of praying to Him?" He might have said the same to Christ—"Why do You pray to One who forsakes You?" But Christ did pray, "My God" still, though He says, "Why dost thou forsake me?" Perhaps Satan tells you not to read the Bible again. It has not comforted you of late. The promises have not come to your soul. Dear beloved, read and read more—read double as much as ever you did. Do not think that because there is no light coming to you, the wisest way is to get away from the light. No; stay where the light is. And perhaps He even says to you, "Don't attend the house of God again. Don't go to the communion table. Why, surely you won't wish to commune with God when He hides His face from you." I say the words of wisdom, for I speak according to the example of Christ. Come still to your God in private and in public worship, and come still, dear friend, to the table of fellowship with Jesus saying, "Though he slay me, yet will I trust in him" (Job 13:15), for I have nowhere else to trust. Though he hide his face from me, yet will I cry after him, and my cry shall not be "My friends," but "My God." My eye shall not look to my soul, my friends, or my feelings, but I will look to my God and even to Him alone. That is the first lesson, not an easy one to learn, mark you—easier to bear than you will find it to practice, but "the Spirit also helpeth our infirmities" (Rom. 8:26). The second lesson is this—observe that:

Though Under a Sense of Desertion, Our Master Does Not Relax His Hold of His God

Observe it, "*My* God"—it is one hand He grips Him with; "*My God*"—it is the other hand He grasps Him with. Both united in the cry, "My God." He believes that God is still His God. He uses the possessive particle twice, "*My* God, *my* God."

Now it is easy to believe that God is ours when He smiles upon us, and when we have the sweet fellowship of His love in our hearts. But the point for faith to attend to, is to hold to God when He gives the hard words, when His providence frowns upon you, and when even His Spirit seems to be withdrawn from you. Oh! let go of everything, but do not let go of God. If the ship be tossed and ready to sink and the tempest rages exceedingly, cast out the ingots, let the gold go, throw out the wheat, as Paul's companions did. Let even necessaries go, but oh! still hold to your God. Do not give up your God. Say still, notwithstanding all, "In the teeth of all my feelings, doubts, and suspicions, I hold Him yet. He is my God, and I will not let Him go."

You know that in the text our Lord calls God in the original His "strong one"—"Eli, Eli"—"my strong one, my mighty one." So let the Christian, when God turns away the brightness of His presence, still believe that all his strength lies in God and that, moreover, God's power is on His side. Though it seemed to crush Him, yet faith says, "It is a power that will not crush me. If He smite me, what will I do? I will lay hold upon His arm, and He will put strength in me. I will deal with God as Jacob did with the angel. If He wrestle with me, I will borrow strength from Him. I will wrestle still with Him until I get the blessing from Him." Beloved, we must neither let go of God, nor let go of our sense of His power to save us. We must hold to our possession of Him and to the belief that He is worth possessing, that He is God all-sufficient, and that He is our God still.

Now I would like to put this personally to any tried child of God here. Are you going to let go of your God because you have lost His smile? Then I ask you, did you base your faith upon His smile? For if you did, you mistook the true ground of faith. The ground of a believer's confidence is not God's smile, but God's promise. It is not His temporary sunshine of His love, but His deep eternal love itself as it reveals itself in the covenant and in the promises. Now the present smile of God may go, but God's promise does not go. If you believe upon is just as true when God frowns as when He smiles. upon the covenant, that covenant is as true in the dark it stands as good when your soul is without a single olation as when your heart is flooded with sacred bliss. ...en to this. The promise is as good as ever. Christ is the same er. His blood is as great a plea as ever. The oath of God is as immutable as ever. We must get away from all building upon our apprehensions of God's love. It is the love itself we must build on—not on our enjoyment of His presence, but on His faithfulness and on His truth. Therefore, be not cast down but still call Him, "My God."

Moreover, I may put it to you, if because God frowns you give Him up, what else do you mean to do? Why, is not it better to trust in an angry God than not to trust in God at all? Suppose you leave off the walk of faith, what will you do? The carnal man never knew what faith was and, therefore, gets on pretty fairly in his own blind, dead way. But you have been quickened and made alive, enlightened. If you give up your faith, what is to become of you! Oh! hold to Him then. Don't give Him up.

> For if thine eye of faith be dim,
> Still hold on Jesus, sink or swim;
> Still at his footstool bow the knee,
> And Israel's God thy strength shall be.

Moreover, if faith gives up her God because He frowns, what sort of a faith was it? Can you not believe in a frowning God? What, have you a friend who the other day gave you a rough word, and you said, "At one time I could die for that man." But because he gives you one rough word, are you going to give him up? Is this your kindness to your friend? Is this your confidence in your God? But how Job played the man! Did he turn against his God when He took away his comforts from him? No; he said, "The LORD gave, and the LORD hath taken away; blessed be the name of the LORD" (1:21). And do you not know how he put it best of all when he said, "Though he slay me, yet will I trust in him" (13:15)? Yes, if your faith be only a fair-weather faith, if you can only walk with God when He sandals you in silver and smoothes the path beneath your feet, what faith is this? Where did you get it from? But the faith that can foot it with the Lord through Nebuchadnezzar's furnace of fire and that can go walking with Him through the valley of the shadow of death, this is the faith to be had and sought after. God grant it to us, for that was the faith that was in the heart of Christ when forsaken of God. He yet says, "My God."

We have learned two lessons. Now that we have learned them (we have gone over them, but have we learned them?), may we practice them, and turn to God in ill times and not relinquish our hold. The third lesson is this:

Although Our Lord Uttered This Deep and Bitter Cry of Pain, Yet Learn from His Silence

He never uttered a single syllable of murmuring or brought any accusation against His God. "*My* God, why hast thou forsaken me?" There! look at those words. Can you see any blots in them? I cannot. They are crystallized sorrow, but there is no defilement of sin. It was just (I was about to say) what an angel could have said if he could have suffered. It is what the Son of God did say, who was purer than angels, when He was suffering. Listen to Job, and we must not condemn Job, for we should not have been half so good as He, I daresay. But he does let his spirit utter itself sometimes in bitterness. He curses the day of his birth and so on; but the Lord Jesus does not do that. There is not a syllable about "cursed be the day in which I was born in Bethlehem, and in which I came among such a rebellious race as this—"no, not a word, not a word. And even the best of men when in sorrow have at least wished that things were not just so. David, when he had lost Absalom, wished that he had died instead of Absalom. But Christ does not appear to want things altered. He does not say, "Lord, this is a mistake. Would God I had died by the hands of Herod when he sought My life, or had perished when they tried to throw Me down the hill of Capernaum." No; nothing of the kind. There is grief, but there is no complaining; there is sorrow, but there is no rebellion.

Now this is the point, beloved, I want to bring to you. If you should suffer extremely, and it should ever come to that terrible pinch that even God's love and the enjoyment of it appears to be gone, put your finger to your lips and keep it there. "I was dumb [with silence], I opened not my mouth; because thou didst it" (Ps. 39:9). Believe that He is a good God still. Know that assuredly He is working for your good, even now, and let not a syllable escape you by way of murmuring, or if it does, repent of it and recall it. You have a right to speak to God, but not to murmur against Him. If you would be like your Lord, you would say just this, "Why hast thou forsaken me?" But you will say no more, and there will you leave Him, and if there come no answer to your question you will be content to be without an answer.

Now again, I say, this is a lesson I can teach, but I do not know if I can practice it. I do not know that you can. Only, again, "the Spirit helpeth also our infirmities," and He will enable us when we come to "lama sabachthani" to come so far, but not to go farther—to stop there with our Lord. The fourth lesson which, I think, we should learn is this:

Our Lord, When He Does Cry,
Cries with the Inquiring Voice of a Loving Child

"My God, *why,* ah! why hast thou forsaken me?" He asks a question not in curiosity, but in love. Loving, sorrowful complaints He brings. "*Why*, my God? Why? Why?" Now this is a lesson to us because we ought to endeavor to fill out why it is that God hides Himself from us. No Christian ought to be content to live without full assurance of faith. No believer ought to be satisfied to live a moment without knowing to a certainty that Christ is his. If he does not know it and assurance is gone, what ought he to do? Why, he should never be content until he has gone to God with the question, "Why have I not this assurance? Why have I not Your presence? Why is it that I cannot live as once I did in the light of Your countenance?" And, beloved, the answer to this question in our case will sometimes be, "I have forsaken you, My child, because you have forsaken me. You have grown cold of heart by slow degrees. Gray hairs have come upon you, and you did not know. I have made you know it to make you see your backsliding and sorrowfully repent of it."

Sometimes the answer will be, "My child, I have forsaken you because you have set up an idol in your heart. You love your child too much, your gold too much, your trade too much. I cannot come into your soul unless I am your Lord, your love, your bridegroom, and your all." Oh! we shall be glad to know these answers because the moment we know them our heart will say—

> The dearest idol I have known,
> Whate'er that idol be,
> Help me to tear it from its throne,
> And worship only thee.

Sometimes the Lord's answer will be, "My child, I have gone from you for a little to try you, to see if you love Me." A true lover will love on under frowns. It is only the superficial professor that wants sweet meats every day, and only loves his God for what he gets out of Him. But the genuine believer loves Him when He smites him, when He bruises him with the bruises of a cruel one. Why, then we will say, "O God, if this is why You do forsake us, we will love You still, and prove to You that Your grace has made our souls to hunger and thirst for You." Depend upon it, the best way to get away from trouble, or to get great help under it, is to run close in to God. In one of Quarles's poems he has the picture of a man striking another with a great flail. Now the further off the other is, the heavier it strikes him. So the man whom God is smiting runs close in, and he cannot be hurt at all. O my God, my God, when away from You affliction stuns me, but I will walk close with You, and then even my affliction I will take to be a cause of glory, and glory in tribulations also, so that Your blast shall not sorely wound my spirit.

Well, I leave this point with the very same remark I made before. To cry to God with the inquiry of a child is the fourth lesson of the text. Oh! learn it well. Do practice it when you are in much trouble. If you are in such a condition at this time, practice it now, and in the pew say, "Show me wherefore thou contendest with me. Search me and try me, and see if there be any wicked way in me, and lead me in the way everlasting." Now the fifth observation is one to be treasured up:

Our Lord, Though He Was Forsaken of God, Still Pursued His Father's Work

Christ pursued the work He came to do. "My God, why hast thou forsaken me?" But, mark you, He does not leave the cross. He does not unloose the nails as He might have done with a will. He did not leap down amidst the assembled mockers and scorn them in return and chase them far away, but He kept on bleeding, suffering, even until He could say, "It is finished." He did not give up the ghost until it was finished. Now, beloved, I find it, and I daresay you do, a very easy and pleasant thing to go on serving God when I have got a full sense of His love—Christ shining in my face, when every text brings joy to my heart, and when I see souls converted, and know that God is going with the Word to bless it. That is very easy, but to keep on serving God when you get nothing for it but blows—when there is no success, and when your own heart is in deep darkness of spirit—I know the temptation. Perhaps you are under it. Because you have not the joy you once had, you say, "I must give up preaching. I must give up that Sunday school. If I have not the light of God's countenance, how can I do it? I must give it up." Beloved, you must do no such thing.

Suppose there were a loyal subject in a nation, and he had done something or other which grieved the king. The king on a certain day turned his face from him, do you think that loyal subject would go away and neglect his duty because the king frowned? No; I think he would say to himself, "I do not know why the king seemed to deal hardly with me. He is a good king, and I know he is good. If he does not see any good in me, I will work for him more than ever. I will prove to him that my loyalty does not depend upon his smiles. I am his loyal subject and will stand to him still." What would you say to your child if you had to chasten him for doing wrong if he were to go away and say, "I shall not attend to the errand that father has sent me upon, and I shall do no more in the house that father has commanded me to do because father has beaten me this morning"? Ah! what a disobedient child! If the scourging had its fit effect upon him, he would say, "I will wrong you no more, father, lest you smite me again." So let it be with us.

Besides, should not our gratitude compel us to go on working for God? Has not He saved us from hell? Then we may say with the old heathen, "Strike, so long as you forgive." Yes, if God forgives, He may strike if He will. Suppose a judge should forgive a malefactor condemned to die, but he should say to him, "Though you are not to be executed as you deserve, yet, for all that, you must be put in prison for some years," he would say, "Ah! my Lord, I will take this lesser chastisement, so long as my life is saved." And oh! if our God has saved us from going down to the pit by putting His own Son to death on our behalf, we will love Him for that if we never have anything more. If, between here and heaven, we should have to say like the elder brother, "Thou never gavest me a kid that I might make merry with my friends," we will love Him still. If He never does anything to us between here and glory but lay us on a sickbed and torture us there, yet still we will praise and bless Him, for He has saved us from going down to the pit. Therefore, we will love Him as long as we live. Oh! if you think of God as you ought to do, you will not be at ups and downs with Him, but you will serve Him with all your heart and soul and might whether you are enjoying the light of his countenance or not.

Now to close. Our Lord is an example for us in one other matter. He is to us our type of what shall happen to us, for whereas He said, "Why hast thou forsaken me?"

He Has Received a Glorious Answer

And so shall every man that in the same spirit in the hour of darkness asks the same question. Our Lord died. No answer had He gotten to the question, but the question went on ringing through earth and heaven and hell. Three days He slept in the grave, and after awhile He went into heaven. And my imagination, I think, may be allowed if I say that as He entered there the echo of His words, "Why hast thou forsaken me?" just died away. Then the Father gave Him the practical answer to the question. For there, all along the golden streets, stood white-robed bands, all of them singing their Redeemer's praise, all of them chanting the name of Jehovah and the Lamb. This was a part of the answer to His question. God had forsaken Christ that these chosen spirits might live through Him. They wore the reward for the travail of His soul. They were the answer to His question. Ever since then, between heaven and earth, there has been constant commerce.

If your eyes were opened that you could see, you would perceive in the sky not falling stars shooting downward, but stars rising upward from England, many every hour from America, from all countries where the Gospel is believed. You would see them from heathen lands where the truth is preached and God is owned. You would see every now and then down on earth a dying bed, but upward through the skies, mounting among the stars, another spirit shot upward to complete the constellations of the glorified. And as these bright ones, all redeemed by His sufferings, enter heaven, they bring to Christ fresh answers to that question, "Why hast thou forsaken me?" And if stooping from His throne in glory the Prince of life takes view of the sons of men who are lingering here, even in this present assembly, He will see tonight a vast number of us met together around this table—I hope the most, if not all of us—redeemed by His blood and rejoicing in His salvation. The Father points down tonight to this Tabernacle, and to thousands of similar scenes where believers cluster around the table of fellowship with their Lord, and He seems to say to the Savior, "There is My answer to Your question, 'Why hast thou forsaken me?'"

Now, beloved, we shall have an answer to our question something like that. When we get to heaven, perhaps not until then, God will tell us why He forsook us. When I tossed upon my bed three months ago in weary pain that robbed me of my night's rest, and my day's rest too, I asked why it was I was there. But I have realized since the reason, for God helped me afterward so to preach that many souls were ingathered. Often you will find that God deserts you that He may be with you after a nobler sort—hides the light, that afterward the light of seven suns at once may break in upon your spirit. There you shall learn that it was for His glory that He left you, for His glory that He tried your faith. Only mind you stand to that. Still cry to Him and still call Him God. Never complain, but ask Him why and pursue His work still under all difficulties, so being like Christ on earth, you shall be like Christ above, as to the answer.

I cannot sit down without saying just this word. God will never forsake His people forever. But as many of you as are not His people, if you have not believed in Him, He will forsake you forever, and forever, and forever. If you ask, "Why hast thou forsaken me?" you will get your answer in the echo of your words, "Thou hast forsaken me." "How shall we escape, if we neglect so great salvation?" (Heb. 2:3). "Believe on the Lord Jesus Christ, and thou shalt be saved" (Acts 16:31).

> But if your ears refuse
>   The language of his grace,
> And hearts grow hard like stubborn Jews,
>   That unbelieving race;
> The Lord in vengeance drest
>   Shall lift his hand and swear,
> "You that despised my promised rest
>   Shall have no portion there."

God grant it may never be so with you, for Christ's sake. Amen.

3

Special Protracted Prayer

*And it came to pass in those days, that he went out into a mountain
to pray, and continued all night in prayer to God (Luke 6:12).*

If any man of woman born might have lived without prayer it was
surely the Lord Jesus Christ. To us poor, weak, erring mortals,
prayer is an absolute necessity. But it does not at first sight seem to
be so to Him who was "holy, harmless, undefiled, separate from sinners" (Heb. 7:26). In some parts of prayer our Lord Jesus Christ could
take no share. As for instance, in that most important department,
namely, personal confession of sin, He could take no portion. There
were no slips in His outward life, there were no declensions in His inward heart. "Forgive us our debts as we forgive our debtors" is a very
suitable prayer for Him to teach us, but He could not use it Himself.
Nor had He any need to pray against inward corruptions, seeing He was
born without them. We wrestle hard each day with original sin, but
Jesus knew no such adversaries. It is as much as we can do, with all the
weapons of our holy war, to keep down the foes of our own household,
but our Lord had no sinful nature to subdue. The inner life is a daily
struggle with some of us, so that Paul's exclamation, "O wretched man
that I am!" (Rom. 7:24), is exceedingly familiar to our lips. But our
Lord said truly of Himself, "The prince of this world cometh, and hath
nothing in me" (John 14:30).

Moreover, our Lord had not to seek some of the things which are exceedingly needful to His disciples. One desire which I trust is ever present with us is for growth in grace and for advancement in the divine
life, but our Lord was always perfect in holiness and love. I see not how
there could have been any advancement in purity in Him. He was always the spotless lily of innocence, incomparable, faultless, without

---

This sermon was taken from *The Metropolitan Tabernacle Pulpit* and was
preached on Sunday morning, March 1, 1868.

spot or wrinkle, or any such thing. Our Lord had no need to make self-examination each night. When He retired for prayer, there would be no need to scan the actions of the day, to detect shortcomings and flaws. There would be no necessity to investigate secret motives to see whether He might not have been actuated by sinister principles. The deep wellsprings of His being were not of earth, but altogether divine. When He bowed His knee in the morning, He had no need to pray to be protected from sin during the day. He went forth to His daily labor without the infirmities which we bear within us and was free from the tendencies to evil which we bear about us. Tempted He was in all points like as we are, but the arrows which wound us glanced harmlessly from Him.

Yet mark you carefully, although our glorious Master did not require to pray in some of those respects in which it is most needful to us, yet never was there a man who was more abundant in prayer and in supplication, nor one in whom prayer was exercised with so much vehemence and importunity. He was the greatest of preachers, but His prayers made even a deeper impression on His disciples than His sermons, for they did not say, "Lord, teach us to preach," but they did exclaim, "Lord, teach us to pray" (Luke 11:1). They felt that He was Master of that heavenly art, and at His feet they desired to sit that they might learn how to move heaven and earth with sacred wrestlings.

Friends, since our sinless Lord was thus mighty in prayer, does not His example say to us, with a voice irresistibly persuasive, "Watch and pray, that ye enter not into temptation" (Matt. 26:41)? You are to be conformed to the image of Christ—be conformed in this respect, that you be men of prayer. You desire to know the secret of His power with men—seek to obtain His power with God. You wish to obtain the blessings which were so copiously bestowed upon Him—seek them where He sought them, find them where He found them. If you would adorn His doctrine and increase His kingdom, use the weapon of all-prayer which ensures victory to all who use it as the Captain did.

Although our Lord Jesus Christ was most constant in His perpetual devotions, yet devout men have been wont to set apart times for extraordinary supplication. A man who does not pray usually is but a hypocrite when He pretends to pray specially. Who would care to live in a miser's house who starved you all the year round, except that now and then on a feast day he fed you daintily? We must not be miserly in prayer, neglecting it regularly, and only abounding in it on particular occasions when ostentation rather than sincerity may influence us. But even He who keeps a bounteous table sometimes spreads a more luxurious feast than at other times. Even so must we, if we habitually live near to God, select our extraordinary seasons in which the soul shall have her fill of fellowship. Our Lord Jesus Christ in the text before us has set us an example of extraordinary devotion, supplying us with all the details and minutiae of the exercise.

Jesus Christ's Example of Prayer

Notice *the place* which He selected for it. He sought the solitude of a mountain. He was so popular that He could not hope in any city or village to be free from innumerable followers. He was so great a benefactor that He could never be without sick folk entreating healing at His hands. He knew no leisure, no, not so much as to eat bread. Therefore, to obtain a little respite, He sought the hollow of some lofty hill where foot of man could not profane His loneliness. If you would draw near to God in an extraordinary manner, you must take care to be entirely undisturbed. I know not how it is, but if ever one desires to approach very near to God, there is sure to be a knock at the door or some matter of urgent business or some untoward circumstance to tempt us from our knees. Is it so, that Satan knows how soul-fattening retirement and devotion are; therefore, if He can by any method stir up friend or foe to call us out our closets, He will surely do so? Here our Lord was beyond call. The mountain was better than a closet with bolted doors. Far off was the din of the city and the noise of those who clamored with their merchandise. Neither the shout of triumph nor the wail of sorrow could reach Him there. Beloved friends, carefully seek if you can a perfect solitude, but if not, reach as near to it as you can. As much as possible keep out the sound and thought of the outer world.

Did not our Lord resort to the mountain in order that He might be able to pray aloud? I cannot speak for others, but I often find it very helpful to myself to be able to speak aloud in private prayer. I do not doubt but that very spiritual minds can pray for a great length of time without the motion of the lips, but I think the most of us would often find it a spur and assistance if we could give utterance to our cries and sights, no one being present to hear. We know that our Lord was accustomed to use strong cryings and tears, and these it would not have been desirable for a human ear to listen to. In fact, His natural modesty would have put Him under a restraint. He therefore sought mountains far away that He might, in His Father's presence and in the presence of no one else, pour out His entire soul—groaning, struggling, wrestling, or rejoicing—as His spirit might be moved at the time.

Did He not also seek the mountain to avoid ostentation? If we pray to be seen of men, we shall have our reward, and a pitiful reward it will be. We shall have the admiration of shallow fools and nothing more. If our object in prayer be to obtain blessings from God, we must present our prayers unspoiled by human observation. Get alone with your God if you would move His arm. If you fast, appear not to men to fast. If you plead personally with God, tell none of it. Take care that this be a secret between God and your own soul, then shall your Father reward you openly. But if you gadabout like a Pharisee to sound your trumpet in the corner of the streets, you shall go where the Pharisee has gone, where hypocrites feel forever the wrath of God.

Jesus, therefore, to prevent interruption, to give Himself the opportunity of pouring out His whole soul, and to avoid ostentation, sought the mountain. What a grand oratory for the Son of God! What walls would have been so suitable? What room would have worthily housed so mighty an intercessor? The Son of God most fittingly entered God's own glorious temple of nature when He would commune with heaven. Those giant hills and the long shadows cast by the moonlight were alone worthy to be His companions. No pomp of gorgeous ceremony can possibly have equaled the glory of nature's midnight on the wild mountain's side where the stars, like the eyes of God, looked down upon the worshiper, and the winds seemed as though they would bear the burden of His sighs and tears upon their willing wings. Samson, in the temple of the Philistines moving the giant pillars, is a mere dwarf compared with Jesus of Nazareth moving heaven and earth as He bows Himself alone in the great temple of Jehovah.

For purposes of extraordinary devotion, the time selected by our Master is also a lesson to us. He chose the silent hours of night. Now, it may so happen, that if we *literally* imitated Him, we might altogether miss our way. No doubt, He chose the night because it was most convenient, congenial, and in every way appropriate. To some of us, the night might be most inappropriate and unsuitable. If so, we must by no means select it, but must follow our Lord in the spirit rather than in the letter. We should give to heavenly things that part of the day in which we can be most quiet, those hours which we can most fairly allot to it without despoiling our other duties of their proper proportion of time.

By day, our Savior was preaching. He could not cease from preaching even to spend the day in prayer. By day the multitude needed healing. Our Lord would not suspend His benevolent work for His private communions. We are to take care never to present one duty to God stained with the blood of another, but to balance and proportion our different forms of service so that our life work may be perfect and entire, wanting nothing. Usually, however, night will be the favored season for wrestling Jacobs. When every man had gone to his own home to rest, the Man of Nazareth had a right to seek His solace where best He could. If sleep refreshed others, and prayer more fully refreshed Him, then by all means let Him pray. Against this not a dog shall move his tongue. Set apart from remarkably protracted intercessions seasons which answer to this description, when the time is your own, not your master's, your own, not your families, not pilfered from family devotion, not abstracted from the public assembly or the Sunday school, the time of quiet when all around you is in repose, the time congenial to solemnity, and the awe of a spirit hushed into reverent subjection, yet uplifted to rapt devotion. Such time, with many, may be the night, with others, it may be the day. Let sanctified common sense be your direction.

Again, our Lord sets us a good example in the matter of extraordinary seasons of devotion in *the protracted character of His prayer*. He continued all night in prayer. I do not think that we are bound to pray long as a general rule. I am afraid, however, there is no great need to make the remark, for the most of Christians are short enough, if not far too short in private worship. By the aid of the Holy Spirit, it is possible to throw by holy energy and sacred zeal as much prayer into a few minutes as into many hours, for prevalent prayer is not measured by God by the yard or by the hour. Force is its standard rather than length. When the whole soul groans itself out in half-a-dozen sentences there may be more real devotion in them than in hours of mere wire drawing and word spinning. True prayer is the soul's mounting up to God, and if it can ride upon a cherub or the wings of the wind so much the better. Yet in extraordinary seasons, when the soul is thoroughly wrought up to an eminent intensity of devotion, it is well to continue it for a protracted season.

We know not that our Lord was vocally praying all the time. He may have paused to contemplate. He may have surveyed the whole compass of the field over which He prayer should extend, meditating upon the character of His God, recapitulating the precious promises, remembering the wants of His people, and thus arming Himself with arguments with which to return to wrestle and prevail. How very few of us have ever spent a whole night in prayer, and yet what boons we might have had for such asking! We little know what a night of prayer would do for us, its effect we can scarcely calculate. One night alone in prayer might make us new men, changed from poverty of soul to spiritual wealth, from trembling to triumphing. We have an example of it in the life of Jacob. Aforetime the crafty shuffler, always bargaining and calculating, unlovely in almost every respect, yet one night in prayer turned the supplanter into a prevailing prince and robed him with celestial grandeur. From that night he lives on the sacred page as one of the nobility of heaven.

Could not we, at least now and then, in these weary earthbound years, hedge about a single night for such enriching traffic with the skies? What, have we no sacred ambition? Are we deaf to the yearning of divine love? Yet, my friends, for wealth and for science men will cheerfully quit their warm couches. Cannot we do it now and then for the love of God and the good of souls? Where is our zeal, our gratitude, our sincerity? I am ashamed while I thus upbraid both myself and you. May we often tarry at Jabbok, and cry with Jacob, as He grasped the angel—

> With thee all night I mean to stay,
> And wrestle till the break of day.

Surely, beloved, if we have given whole days to folly, we can afford a space for heavenly wisdom. Time was when we gave whole nights to chambering and wantonness, to dancing and the world's revelry. We did not tire then. We were chiding the sun that he rose so soon, and wishing the hours would lag awhile that we might delight in wilder merriment, and perhaps deeper sin. Oh, wherefore, should we weary in our heavenly employment? Why grow we weary when asked to watch with our Lord? Up, sluggish heart, Jesus calls you! Rise and go forth to meet the heavenly friend in the place where He manifests Himself.

Jesus has further instructed us in the art of special devotion by *the manner of His prayer*. Notice, He continued all night in prayer *to God—to God*. How much of our prayer is not prayer *to God* at all! It is nominally so, but it is really a muttering to the winds, a talking to the air, for the presence of God is not realized by the mind. "He that cometh to God must believe that he is, and that he is a rewarder of them that diligently seek him" (Heb. 11:6). Do you know what it is mentally to lay hold upon the great unseen One and to talk with Him as really as you talk to a friend whose hand you grip? How heavenly to speak right down into God's ear, to pour your heart directly into God's heart, feeling that you live in Him as the fish live in the sea, and that your every thought and word are discerned by Him. It is true pleading when the Lord is present to you, and you realize His presence, and speak under the power and influence of His divine overshadowing.

That is to pray indeed, but to continue all night in such a frame of mind is wonderful to me. I must confess, and I suppose it is your confession too, that if for awhile I get near to God in prayer, yet distracting thoughts will intrude, the ravenous birds will come down upon the sacrifice, the noise of archers will disturb the songs at the place of drawing of water. How soon do we forget that we are speaking to God and go on mechanically pumping up our desires, perhaps honestly uttering them, but forgetting to whom they are addressed! Oh, were He not a gracious God, the imperfection of our prayers would prevent so much as one of them even reaching His ears. But He knows our frailty and takes our prayers, not as what they are, but as what we mean them to be, and, beholding them in Jesus Christ, He accepts both us and them in the Beloved. Do let us learn from our Master to make our prayers distinctly and directly appeals to God. That gunner will do no service to the army who takes no aim, but is content so long as he does but fire. That vessel makes an unremunerative voyage which is not steered for a port, but is satisfied to sail hither and thither. We must direct our prayers to God and maintain soul-fellowship with Him, or our devotion will become a nullity, a name for a thing which is not.

The Ethiopic translation reads "in prayer *with God*." Truly this is the highest order of prayer. Though the translation may be indefensible, the meaning is correct enough, for Jesus was eminently with God all night. To pray with God, do you know what that is? To be the echo of Jehovah's voice! To desire the Lord's desires and long with His longings! This is a gracious condition to be in, when the heart is a tablet for the Lord to write upon, a coal blazing with celestial fire, a leaf driven with the heavenly wind. Oh, to be absorbed in the divine will, having one's whole swallowed up in the mind of God! This for a whole night would be blessed; this forever bliss itself.

Note too, that some have translated the passage "in the prayer *of God*." This is probably an incorrect translation, though Dr. Gill appears to endorse it, but it brings out a precious meaning. The most eminent things were in the Hebrew language ascribed to God, so that by it would be meant the noblest prayer, the most intense prayer, the most vehement prayer. A prayer in which the whole man gathers up his full strength and spends it in an agony before the eternal throne. Oh, to pray like that! The great, deep, vehement prayer of God! Friends, I am afraid that as a rule in our prayer meetings, we are much too decorous, and even in our private prayers feel too much the power of formality. Oh! how I delight to listen to a brother who talks to God simply and from his heart. I must confess I have no small liking to those rare old-fashioned Methodist prayers that are now quite out of date. Our Methodist friends, for the most part, are getting too fine and respectable nowadays, too genteel to allow of prayers such as once made the walls to ring again. O for a revival of those glorious violent prayers that flew like hot shot against the battlements of heaven! O for more moving of the posts of the doors in vehemence; more thundering at the gates of mercy! I would sooner attend a prayer meeting where there were groans and cries all over the place, and cries and shouts of "Hallelujah!" than be in your polite assembles where everything is dull as death and decorous as the whitewashed sepulcher. O for more of the prayer of God, the whole body, soul, and spirit working together, the whole man being aroused and stirred up to the highest pitch of intensity to wrestle with the Most High! Such, I have no doubt, the prayer of Jesus was on the cold mountain's side.

The Occasion for His Prayer

Once more, we may learn from Jesus our Lord *the occasion* for special devotion. At the time when our Master continued all night in prayer He had been upbraided by the Pharisees. He fulfilled the resolve of the man after God's own heart. "Let the proud be ashamed; for they dealt perversely with me without cause: but I will meditate in thy precepts." So David did, and so did David's Lord. The best answer to the slanderers of the ungodly is to be more constant in communion with God. Now, has it been so with any of you? Have you been persecuted or despised? Have you passed through any unusual form of trial? Then celebrate an unusual season of prayer. This is the alarm bell which God rings. Haste to Him for refuge. See to it that in this your time of trouble you betake yourself to the mercy seat with greater diligence.

Another reason is also noticed in the context. Christ had said to His disciples, "Pray ye therefore the Lord of the harvest, that He will send forth labourers into his harvest" (Matt. 9:38). What He told them to do He would be sure to do Himself. He was just about to choose twelve apostles, and before that solemn act of ordination was performed, he sought power for them from the Most High. Who can tell what blessings were vouchsafed to the Twelve in answer to that midnight intercession? If Satan fell like lightning from heaven, Jesus' prayer did it rather than the apostles' preaching. So, Christian man, if you enter upon a new enterprise, or engage in something that is weightier and more extensive than what you have done before, select a night or a day, and set it apart for special communion with the Most High. If you are to pray, you must work, but if you are to work, you must also pray. If your prayer without your work will be hypocrisy, your work without your prayer will be presumption. So see to it that you are specially in supplication when specially in service. Balance your praying and working, and when you have reached the full tale of the one, do not diminish any of the other.

To any man here who asks me, "When should I give myself especially to a protracted season of prayer?" I would answer, these occasions will frequently occur. You should certainly do this when about to join the church. The day of your profession of your faith publicly should be altogether a consecrated day. I recollect rising before the sun to seek my Master's presence on the day when I was buried with Him in baptism. It seemed to me a solemn and earnest manner. What is baptism without fellowship with Christ? To be buried in baptism, but not *with Him,* what is it? I would say to you young people who are joining the church now, mind you do not do it thoughtlessly, but in coming forward to enlist in the army of Christ, set apart a special

season for self-examination and prayer. When you arrive at any great
change of life do the same. Do not enter upon marriage, or upon
emigration, or upon starting in business without having sought a
benediction from your Father who is in heaven. Any of these things
may involve years of pain or years of happiness to you. Seek, therefore,
to have the smile of God upon what you are about to do.

Should you not also make your times of peculiar trial to be also
times of special prayer? Wait upon God now that the child is dying.
Wrestle with Him as David did about the child of Bathsheba. Draw
near to God with fasting and prayer for a life that is specially dear to
you if perhaps it may be preserved. When the ax of death falls and the
tree beneath which you found shelter is cut down, then again before the
grave is closed, and the visitation is forgotten, draw near to God with
sevenfold earnestness. And if you have been studying the Word of God,
and cannot master a passage of Scripture, if some truth of revelation
staggers you, now again is a time to set yourself like Daniel by prayer
and supplication to find out what is the meaning of the Lord in the book
of His prophecy.

Indeed, such occasions will often occur to you who are spiritual. I
charge you by the living God, if you would be rich in grace, if you
would make great advances in the divine life, if you would be eminent
in the service of your Master, attend to these occasions. Get an hour
alone, an hour, aye, two hours a day if you can, and go not away from
the Master's presence until your face is made to shine as once the face
of Moses did when He had been long upon the mount alone with God.

And now having thus brought out the example of Christ as well as I
can, I want to make an application of the subject to this church, which
at this juncture has set apart a long season for special devotion. My
words shall be few, but I earnestly desire that God may make them
weighty to each member of this church.

An Application to the Church

A church, in order to have a blessing upon its special times of
prayer, must abound in constant prayer at other times. I do not believe
in spasmodic efforts for revival. There should be special occasions, but
these should be the outgrowths of ordinary, active, healthy vigor. To neglect prayer all the year round, and then to celebrate a special week, is
it much better than hypocrisy? To forsake the regular prayer meetings,
but to come in crowds to a special one, what is this? Does it not betray
superficiality or the effervescence of mere excitement? The church
ought always to pray. Prayer is to her what salt and bread are to our ta-
bles. No matter what the meal, we must have salt and bread there, and
no matter what the church's engagements, she must have her regular

constancy of prayer. I think that in London our churches err in not having morning and evening prayer daily in every case where the church is large enough to maintain it. I am glad that our zealous members have here for some years maintained that constant prayer. I am thankful that in this church I cannot find much fault with you for non-attendance at the prayer meetings. There are some of you who never come, and I suppose you are such poor things that you are not of much good whether you come or stay away. But on the whole, the most of the people who fear God in this place are abundant in their attendance at the means of grace, not to be blamed in any measure whatever for forsaking the assembling of themselves together, for they do draw near to God most regularly. Such prayer meetings have we every Monday, as I fear are not to be found anywhere else. But we must see to it that we keep this up. Moreover, those who are lax and lagging behind, must ask forgiveness of their heavenly Father, and endeavor henceforth to be more instant in supplication.

If *men and women* ought always to pray and not to faint, much more *Christian men and women*. Jesus has sent His church into the world on the same errand upon which He Himself came, and that includes intercession. What if I say that the church is the world's priest? Creation is dumb, but the church is to find a mouth for it. Ungodly men are dumb of heart and will, but we who have the will and the power to intercede dare not be silent. It is the church's privilege to pray. The door of grace is always open for her petitions, and they never return empty-handed. The veil was rent for her, the blood was sprinkled upon the altar for her, God constantly invites her. Will she refuse the privilege which angels might envy her? Is not the church the bride of Christ? May she not go in to her King at any time, at every time? Shall she allow the precious privilege to be unused? The church ever has need for prayer. There are always some in her midst who are declining, and frequently those who are falling into open sin. There are the lambs to be prayed for that they may be carried in Christ's bosom. There are the strong to be prayed for lest they grow presumptuous, and the weak lest they become despairing. In such a church as this is, if we kept up prayer meetings twenty-four hours in the day, three hundred sixty-five days in the year, we might never be without a special subject for supplication. Are we ever without the sick and the poor? Are we ever without the afflicted and the watering? Are we ever without those who are seeking the conversion of their relatives, the reclaiming of backsliders, or the salvation of the depraved? No, with such congregations constantly gathering; with such a densely peopled neighborhood; with three million sinners around us, the most part of them lying dead in trespasses and sins; with such a country beginning to be benighted in superstition, over whom the darkness of Romanism is certainly gathering; in a world full of idols, full of cruelties, full of devilries, if the church does not pray, how shall she excuse her base neglect of the command of her loving Lord and covenant head? Let this church then be constant in supplication.

There should be frequent prayer meetings. These prayer meetings should be constantly attended by all. Every man should make it a point of duty to come as often as possible to the place where prayer is wont to be made. I wish that all throughout this country the prayers of God's churches were more earnest and constant. It might make a man weep tears of blood to think that in our dissenting churches in so many cases the prayer meetings are so shamefully attended. I could indicate places that I know of, situated not many miles from where we now stand, where there are sometimes so few in attendance that there are scarcely praying men enough to keep up variety in the prayer meeting. I know towns where the prayer meeting is put off during the summer months as if the Devil would be put off during the summer! I know of agricultural districts where they are always put off during the harvest. I make some kind of excuse for them because the fruits of the earth must be gathered in. But I cannot understand large congregations where the prayer meeting and lecture are amalgamated because there will not be enough persons coming out to make two decent services in the week. And then they say that God does not bless the Word. How can He bless the Word?

They say, "Our conversions are not so numerous as they were," and they wonder how it is that we at the Tabernacle have so large an increase month by month. Do you wonder that they have not a blessing when they do not seek it? Do you wonder that we have it when we do seek it? That is but a natural law of God's own government, that if men will not pray, neither shall they have. If men will pray, and pray vehemently, God will deny them nothing. He opens wide His hand and says, "Ask what ye will, and it shall be given to you." I wish our denomination of Baptist and other denominations of Christians were greater believers in prayer, for this mischief of Ritualism and Rationalism which is coming upon us, this curse which is withering our nation, this blight and mildew which is devouring the vineyard of the Lord, has all come upon us because public prayer has almost ceased in the land as to its constancy, vehemence, and importunity. The Lord recover us from this sin!

But let the church be as diligent in prayer as she may on regular occasions, she ought still to have her special seasons. A thing which is regular and constant is sure to tire, and a little novelty is lawful. A little speciality may often tend to revive those who, otherwise, would be given to slumber. The church should have her special praying times because she has her special needs. There are times when spiritual epidemics fall upon churches and congregations. Sometimes it is the disease of pride, luxury, worldliness. At other times there are many falling into overt sin. Sometimes a black form of vice will break out in the very midst of the church of God. At other times it is a heresy or a doctrine carried to excel, or ill-will, or a want of brotherly love, or a general lethargy. At such special times of trial a church should have her extraordinary prayer meetings. As also when she is engaging in new enterprises and is about to break up new ground, she needs fresh strength and should seek it. Let her call her members together, and with heart and soul let them commend the work to God.

There should be special seasons of prayer because the Holy Spirit prompts us to it. "I believe in the Holy Ghost," is a sentence of the Creed, but how few do really believe it! We seem to fancy that we have no motions of the Holy Spirit now among godly men as aforetime. But I protest before the living God that such is not the case. The Holy Spirit at this day moves in those who are conversant with Him, and who are content to regard His gracious monitions, and He prompts us to especial fellowship. We speak what we do know, we declare what we have tasted and handled. The Holy Spirit, at certain times, prompts us to come together with peculiar earnestness and special desires. And then, if this suffice not, God has been pleased to set His seal to special seasons of prayer, therefore they ought to be held.

There have been more ingatherings, I was about to say, under the special efforts of a month than under ordinary efforts of eleven months. I am sure that last year we saw very clearly God's blessing upon us during the month of February. All the year round—my dear brethren, the deacons and elders, can bear me out in it—there were always cases coming forward who said, "We were decided for Christ during the February meetings." God has always blessed the ministry here. I say it, not to boast, but to the glory to God. I do not know of any sermon preached here without conversions. But yet those times of special meeting, those solemn assemblies, have always been a hundredfold blessed of God, so that we have good reason to say we will continue them with renewed zeal because the Lord is with them.

Now, friends, I must have just a word with you upon another matter, namely, that *it should be our endeavor to bring power into these special meetings.* They are lawful, they are necessary, let us make them profitable. The way to do so is to draw near to God as Christ did. When He prayed, it was a Son talking to His Father, the Son of God talking with the Father God, and unbosoming His heart in close communion. Come up tomorrow, my friends, as sons and daughters of God to your Father. Speak to Him as to one who is very near akin to you. There will be no lack of power if such be the case. Jesus drew near to God in His prayer as a priest, the High Priest making intercession for the people. You are all priests and kings to God, if you believe in Christ. Come with your breastplates on tomorrow; come that you may intercede before the throne, pleading the merit of the precious blood. There will be no flagging if every man put on his priestly miter. Jesus came before God with a burning zeal for His Father's glory. He could say, "The zeal of thine house hath eaten me up" (Ps. 69:9). Burn and blaze, my friends, with love to God. Wait upon Him this afternoon, let that be a special private season of prayer, and ask Him to teach you how to love Him, show you how to reverence Him, and fire you with an intense ambition to spread abroad the savor of His name. Jesus Christ drew near to God in prayer with a wondrous love to the sons of men. Those tears of His were not for Himself but for others. Those sighs and cries were not for His own pangs, but for the sorrows and the sins of men. Try to feel as Christ did. Get a tender heart, an awakened conscience, quickened sympathies, and then if you come up to the house of God, the prayer meetings cannot be dull.

Seek to be bathed in the blood of Christ. Go, my friends, to the wounds of Christ and get life blood for your prayers. Sit you down at Golgotha and gaze upon your dying Lord, and hear Him say, "I have loved you, and given Myself for you." Then rise up with this resolve in your soul—

> Now for the love I bear his name,
> What was my gain I count my loss,

and go forward determined in His strength that nothing shall be wanting on your part to win for Him a kingdom, to gain for Him the hearts of the sons of men. If such shall be your state of mind, I am quite sure there will be power with God in prayer.

In closing, I shall say to you, we, above all the churches of this country, have a special need and a special encouragement to make our prayers things of power. For, in the first place, my friends, what a multitude we now are! I often wish, though I beg to be pardoned of the Lord for it, that I had never occupied the position that I now fill because of its solemn responsibilities. I tell you, when I feel them they crush me to the ground, and I can only manage to sustain my spirits by endeavoring to cast them upon the Lord. Why, three thousand seven hundred of you in church fellowship, or thereabouts, what can *I* do? Somebody complains that this sick one is not visited or that that sinning one is not rebuked. How can I do it? How can one man, how can twenty men, how can a hundred men do the work? God knows I would, if I could, cut myself in pieces, that every piece might be active in His service. But how can we rule and minister fully in such a church as this? God has supplied my lack of service very wonderfully. Still there are things that make my heart ache day and night, as well as other matters that make my soul to leap for joy. O pray for this great church! Where our power utterly fails us, let us implore the divine power to come in that all may be kept right. We have need to pray, for some have fallen. We have to confess it with a blush that crimsons our cheek, some have fallen shamefully. O pray that others may not fall, and that the good men and true among us may be upheld by the power of God through faith to salvation.

Think of the agencies which we are employing. If we do not pray for these they will be so much wasted effort. Every week the sermons preached here are scattered by tens of thousands all over the globe, not in this language only, but in all the languages of Christendom are they read. Pray that God's blessing may rest upon the Word which He has blessed aforetime. Our sons, our young ministers whom this church has trained at her feet, now are to be counted by hundreds, scattered all over this country and elsewhere. Intercede for them. Forget not your own sons, turn not your hearts away from your own children whom God has sent forth to be heralds of the Cross. In your Sunday schools, in your tract distributions, in your city missions, in your street preaching, in your colportage, in your orphanage, everywhere you are seeking to glorify Christ. Do not, I beseech you, forget the one thing needful in all this. Do not be foolish builders, who will buy marble and precious stones at great cost, and then forget to lay the cornerstone securely. If it is worthwhile to serve God, it is worthwhile to pray that the service may be blessed. Why all this labor and cost? It is but offering to the Lord that which He cannot accept, except by prayer you sanctify the whole. I think I see you as a church standing by the side of your altar with the victims slain and the wood placed in order, but there is as yet still wanting the fire from on high. O intercede, you Elijahs, men of like passions with us, but yet earnest men, upon whose hearts God has written prayer—intercede mightily! until at last the fire shall come down from heaven to consume the sacrifice and to make all go up like a pillar of smoke to the Most High.

I cannot speak to you as I would. The earnestness of my heart prevents my lips uttering what I feel. But if there be any bonds of love between us, above all, if there be any bonds of love between us and Christ, by His precious blood, by His death-sweat, by His holy life, and by His agonizing death, I do beseech you to strive together with us in your prayers that the Spirit of God may rest upon us, and to God shall be the glory. Amen and Amen.

4

The Joy of Jesus

*In that hour Jesus rejoiced in spirit, and said, I thank thee, O Father,
Lord of heaven and earth, that thou hast hid these things from the
wise and prudent, and hast revealed them unto babes: even so,
Father; for so it seemed good in thy sight. All things are delivered to
me of my Father: and no man knoweth who the Son is, but the
Father; and who the Father is, but the Son, and he to whom the Son
will reveal him (Luke 10:21–22).*

Last Lord's day morning we considered the lamentations of
Jesus. We will now turn our thoughts to the joys of Jesus. It is
remarkable that this is the only instance on record in the
gospels in which our Lord is said to have rejoiced. It stands alone, and
is, therefore, the more to be prized: "In that hour Jesus rejoiced in
spirit." He was the "man of sorrows and acquainted with grief" for our
sakes, and therefore we are not astonished to find few indications of
joy in the story of His life. Yet I do not think it would be fair to infer
from the fact of a solitary mention of His rejoicing that He did not rejoice at other times. On the contrary, our Lord must, despite His sorrow, have possessed a peaceful, happy spirit. He was infinitely
benevolent and went about doing good. Benevolence always finds a
quiet delight in blessing others. The joy of the lame when they leaped
and of the blind when they saw must have gladdened the soul of Jesus.
To cause happiness to others must bring home to a sympathetic bosom
some degree of pleasure. Sir Philip Sydney was wont to say, "Doing
good is the only certainly happy action of a man's life." Assuredly it is
hard to see how the love of Jesus could refrain from rejoicing in blessing those around Him.

Moreover, our Lord was so *pure* that He had a well of joy within

---

This sermon was taken from *The Metropolitan Tabernacle Pulpit* and was
preached on Sunday morning, December 5, 1880.

which could not fail Him. If it be indeed true that virtue is true happiness, then Jesus of Nazareth was happy. The poet said—

> What nothing earthly gives, or can destroy,
> The soul's calm sunshine and the heartfelt joy,
> Is virtue's prize.

Such calm and joy must have been the Savior's, though for our sake He bowed beneath the heavy load of sorrow. The perfectly holy God is the perfectly happy God. The perfectly Holy Christ, had it not been that He had taken upon Himself our griefs and sicknesses, would have been perfectly happy. But even with our griefs and sicknesses there must have been a deep peace of soul within Him that sustained Him in His deepest woe. Did not the Father Himself say of His beloved Son, "Thou lovest righteousness, and hatest wickedness: therefore God, thy God, hath anointed thee with the oil of gladness above thy fellows" (Ps. 45:7)?

Nor is this all, for our blessed Lord lived in unbroken fellowship with the Father. Fellowship with God will not permit a soul to abide in darkness, for, walking with God, he walks in the light as God is in the light. Such a mind may, for certain purposes, come under clouds and glooms. But light is sown for the righteous, and it will speedily break forth as the dawn of day. Those nights of prayer and days of perfect service must have brought their own calm to the tried heart of the Son of God.

Besides, Christ Jesus was a man of *faith*—faith's highest exposition and example. He is "the author and the finisher of our faith" (Heb. 12:2), in whom we see its life, walk, and triumph. Our Lord was the incarnation of perfect confidence in the Father. In His life all the histories of great believers are summed up. Read Hebrews 11 and see the great cloud of witnesses. Then mark how in the twelfth chapter Paul bids us look to Jesus as though in His person the whole multitude of the witnesses could be seen. He it was, who "for the joy that was set before him endured the cross, despising the shame" (Heb. 12:2). His faith must, therefore, have anticipated the reward of His passion, and have brought the joy thereof home to Him even while He sorrowed here. His joy was a light from the lamps of the future that were to be kindled by His death and victory. He had meat to eat that His disciples knew not of, for His long-sighted eye saw further than they. While they mourned His departure, He saw the expediency of it, and told them that if they loved Him they would rejoice because He was going to the Father. Be sure of this, that our Lord felt beneath the great water floods of outward affliction an undercurrent of joy, for He said, "These things have I spoken unto you, that my joy might remain in you, and that your joy might be full" (John 15:11). What meant He by this if He had no joy in His people? Could He have spoken so many happy words, and so often have said to His disciples, "Be of good cheer," if He had been always downcast Himself?

But still it is remarkable that our text should be the sole recorded instance of His joy, so far as the evangelists are concerned. It is clear that joy was not a distinguishing feature in our Lord's life, so as to strike the beholder. Peace may have sat serenely on His brow, but nothing of the exuberant spirits which are seen in some men, for His countenance was marred with lines of care and grief. We do not hear that He laughed, though it is thrice recorded that He wept. Here for once, as quite unique, we find the inspired assurance that He rejoiced. Because of its singularity the record deserves to be looked into with care that we may see the cause of delight so unusual.

The words here used are very emphatic. "He rejoiced." The Greek word is much stronger than the English rendering. It signifies "to leap for joy." It is the word of the blessed Virgin's song, "My spirit hath rejoiced in God my Saviour" (Luke 1:47). Strong emotions of delight were visible upon our Lord's face, and were expressed by the tones of His voice, as well as by His words. It is clear that He was greatly glad. The text also says He *"rejoiced in spirit."* That is, deep down in the very center of His nature, in that largest and most capacious part of His human being, the Redeemer rejoiced. Man is body, soul, and spirit. But the spirit is the nobler and most vital part, and it was with a spiritual, inward, and most living joy that the Lord Jesus Christ rejoiced. It was joy of the truest and finest sort that made the Savior's heart to dance. Come we, then, near to this rejoicing Savior, who wraps the garments of praise about Him, perfumed with delight. Let us see if we cannot learn somewhat from His joys, since, I trust, we gathered something from His griefs.

Joy in the Father's Revelation of the Gospel

"I thank thee, O Father, . . . that thou hast hid these things from the wise and prudent, and hast revealed them unto babes." He rejoices in His Father's revelation of the Gospel. It was not joy in the fame which had gathered about His name inasmuch that John heard of it in prison. It was not joy in the manifest tokens of power that went forth with His commissioners, though they rejoiced that devils were subject to them. But it was joy in God's revealing the Gospel to the sons of men.

I call your attention to the fact that He ascribed all that was done to the Father, *and joyed that the Father was walking with Him.* His disciples came back to Him and said, "Even the devils are subject unto us through thy name" (Luke 10:17). They spoke not amiss, for the name of

Jesus was their strength and deserved honor. But the Lord, with that sacred self-abnegation which was so natural to Him, replies, "I thank thee, O Father, that thou hast revealed these things." He takes no honor to Himself, but ascribes the glory to the Father, who wrought with Him. Imitate Him, O you who call Him Lord! Let the work of the Father be your joy. If God gives us any success in the preaching of the Gospel let our joy be that the Father's power is going forth with the Word. We are not so much to joy in our instrumentality as in the hand which uses the instrument and works by it. Oh, misery, misery! to be attempting Gospel ministry without God! But oh, bliss, bliss unspeakable, to feel that when we lift our hand God's hand is lifted too. When we speak the Word the voice of God is ringing through our feeble speech and reaching the hearts of men! It is to true believers a great joy that the Father is bringing home His wandering children and receiving penitents into His bosom.

The Savior's joy was that through the Father's grace *men were being enlightened.* The seventy disciples had been from city to city working miracles and preaching the Gospel, and their Master was glad when they returned with tidings of success: "In that hour Jesus rejoiced in spirit." It pleases Jesus when the Gospel has free course, and God is glorified thereby. Then, in measure, He sees of the travail of His soul and is filled with satisfaction. Shall we not find our joy where He finds His? Shall we not enter into the joy of our Lord? Whenever we hear good news of a village evangelized, of a township moved by the glad tidings, of a country long shut up from the Gospel at length opened to the Word, let us feel our highest and deepest joy. Rather let us rejoice in this than in business prosperity or personal advantage. What if we can find no joy in our own circumstances, what if even spiritual affairs within our soul are full of difficulty? Let us joy and rejoice that God the Father is revealing the light of His Gospel among the sons of men. Be this our highest wish, "Thy kingdom come" (Matt. 6:10; Luke 11:2), and in that coming kingdom let us find our most happiness. Be sure that the joy that warmed the heart of Christ can do us no hurt. It must be a pure, sacred, and ennobling joy; therefore let us indulge in it very largely. Christ's joy lay in the Father's sending forth His light and His truth, making men to see things which prophets and kings had desired to behold, but had not been favored to see. Jesus rejoiced in this, that the blessings of grace were being revealed by the Father.

Further, our Savior's joy lay very much in this, that this revelation to men *was being made through such humble instruments.* We read that "he lifted up his eyes on his disciples, and said, Blessed be ye poor: for yours is the kingdom of God" (Luke 6:20). There was not among the Twelve or the Seventy one person of any social status. They were the common people of the field and the sea. In after years Paul was raised up, a man richly endowed in learning, whose great abilities were used by the Lord. But the first ministers of Christ were a band of fishermen and countrymen, altogether unknown in the schools of learning and regarded as "unlearned and ignorant men" (Acts 4:13). The grandest era in the world's history was ushered in by nobodies. By persons who, like their leader, were despised and rejected of men. To any one of them it might have been said, "For ye see your calling, brethren, how that not many wise men after the flesh, not many mighty, not many noble, are called: but God hath chosen the foolish things of the world to confound the wise; and God hath chosen the weak things of the world to confound the things which are mighty; and base things of the world, and things which are despised, hath God chosen, yea, and things which are not, to bring to nought things that are: that no flesh should glory in his presence" (1 Cor. 1:26–29).

Observe carefully that the persons whom our Lord had been employing were not only obscure in origin, but they were of a low degree of spiritual understanding. They were in fact babes in grace as well as worldly wisdom. Their joy, when they came back to tell what had been done, was evidently childish as well as gracious. They joyed in their success as children do in their little achievements. But their Lord was thankful because He saw the openheartedness and the simplicity of their characters in the gladsome way in which they cried, "Lord, even the devils are subject unto us through thy name" (Luke 10:17). He thanked God that by such babes as these, such children, such true-hearted children, and yet such mere children, He was pleased to make known His Word among the sons of men. Rest assured that our Lord even at this day finds a delight in the weakness of the instruments He uses.

> He takes the fool and makes him know
> The mysteries of his grace;
> To bring aspiring wisdom low,
> And all its pride abase.

Not you, you scribes, who have counted every letter of the Old Testament, does He elect to be filled with the Spirit. Not you, you Pharisees, who so abound in outward religion, does He choose to spread the inward life and light. Not you, you Sadducees, who are versed in skeptical philosophy and boast your cleverness, does He call to preach His Gospel to the poor. He has taken to be the heralds of His glory men from the sea of Galilee whom you despise. Men who are simple-hearted, ready to learn, and then as ready to tell out again the message of Salvation. Our Lord was by no means displeased with the absence of culture and learning in His followers, for the culture and learning of the period were utter vanity, but He was glad to see that they did not pretend to wisdom or astuteness, but came to Him in all simplicity to accept His teaching because they believed Him to be the Son of God. Jesus rejoiced in spirit about this.

And yet, further, His great joy was *that the converts were of such a character* as they were. "Thou hast hid these things from the wise and prudent, and hast revealed them unto babes." It is true that certain persons sneeringly asked, "Have any of the rulers or the Pharisees believed in Him?" There were some who thought lightly of Jesus because those whom they imagined to be learned men had not signified their adhesion to His cause. Our Lord Himself had no concern in that direction, but called the Pharisees blind and the scribes hypocrites, as they assuredly were. Other voices may have inquired, "Who are these that follow Jesus? Of what class are His converts?" The answer would have been, "They are rustics, fishermen, and common people with here and there a woman of substance and a man of means. The bulk of them are the poor to whom for the first time the Gospel is preached. Such have gathered to Christ and received His Word." Some even said that a parcel of boys and girls were in the streets crying, "Hosanna," and this showed how commonplace the Preacher was. At this day I have heard the Lord's people spoken of as a poor set—people of no position, a lot of persons whose names will never be known, a mere assembly of Jack, Tom, Harry, Mary, Susan, and the rest. This was the very thing to which Jesus refers with thankfulness. He was glad that He was surrounded by unsophisticated, childlike natures, rather than by Pharisees and scribes, who, even if they be converted, are sure to bring some of their old manners with them.

He was glad that the Father had revealed His light and His salvation to those who were lowly and humble, who, though poor in this world, were "strong in faith, giving glory to God" (Rom. 4:20). Thus you see that the very fact which certain very superior people fling in our teeth as a disgrace was to our Savior a subject of joy. I have heard foolish ones sneer at certain churches that are earnest for the truth by affectedly asking, "Who are they? A mob of common people, tradesmen or working men, and the like. Are there any of the aristocracy among them? Do you find any of the highly intellectual in their ranks?" What if we do not, we shall not therefore sorrow, but join with Jesus in saying, "We thank thee, O Father, that thou hast hid these things from the wise and prudent, and hast revealed them unto babes." Christ found Himself at home among those openhearted folks that gathered around Him, for He was Himself a child-man who wore His heart upon his sleeve, boasting of no wisdom though He was wisdom's self. Our Lord never sought

Himself as the wise and prudent of His age did. But He was meek and lowly in heart, and therefore found Himself at home among a people who were willing to receive His teaching and eager to tell it out again to their countrymen. So He blessed and praised God that such were chosen. Oh, friends, it is not that Christ would not have the greatest come to Him, it is not that Christ would not have the learned come to Him; but so it is, that His greatest joy is that those come who, whatever the greatness or the littleness of their learning, are childlike in spirit, and like babes are willing to learn and are prepared to receive what He shall teach to them. He was glad to receive persons with lowly notions of their own intelligence, and a supreme belief in the veracity of their great Teacher.

If those who are reckoned to be learned profess to come to Christ, they are generally a trial to the church. All the merely human learning that has ever come to the church has, as a rule, been mischievous to it. It always needs great grace to keep it in its right place. At first came the Gnostics with their philosophy, and into what perils they dragged the church of God I cannot stay to tell you. Then arose others out of whose wisdom grew Arianism, and the church was well-nigh withered to her very heart by that deadly form of heresy. The schoolmen did for her much the same, and to this day whenever any of the would-be-thought-wise men meddle with religion, they tell us that the plain Word of God, as we read it, must be interpreted by modern thought. That it bears another meaning which only the cultured can possibly comprehend. When philosophy invades the domain of revelation it ends in perverting the Gospel, and in bringing in "another gospel which is not another." It is with human wisdom as it is with human riches, how hardly shall they that have it enter into the kingdom of God! True wisdom is another thing—that is a gift which comes from above and causes no puffing up of the heart, for it adores the God from whom it came. The wisdom which is true and real the Lord is prepared to give to those who confess their unwisdom, to those who will be babes in His sight. It is not ignorance that God loves, but conceit that He hates. Knowledge is good, but the affectation of it is evil. O for more true wisdom! May God give us much of it, and may those who are babes as yet come to be men of full stature in Christ Jesus. Yet forget not your Lord's joy in the character of His converts, but remember the lines in which the poet of the sanctuary paraphrases our text:

> Jesus, the man of constant grief
> A mourner all his days,
> His Spirit once rejoiced aloud,
> And turned his joy to praise.

Father, I thank thy wondrous love,
That hath revealed thy Son
To men unlearned, and to babes
Hath made thy gospel known.

The mysteries of redeeming grace
Are hidden from the wise,
While pride and carnal reasoning join
To swell and blind their eyes.

Our Lord's joy sprang from one other source, namely, His view of *the manner in which God was pleased to save His people*. It was by *revealing* these things to them. There is, then, to every man who is saved a revelation, not of anything over and above what is given us in the Word of God, but of that same truth to himself personally and with power. In the Word is the light. But what is needed is that each man's eye should be opened by the finger of God to see it. Truth in the Scriptures will never save until it becomes truth in the heart. It must be "revealed" to the most unprejudiced and true-hearted. Even men of childlike spirits and receptive natures will not see the truth unless it be specially revealed to them. There must be a work of the Father through the Holy Spirit upon each intellect and mind before it can perceive the truth as it is in Jesus. Hence, when unregenerate men tell us that they cannot see the beauty of the Gospel, we are not at all astonished—we never thought they could. When boastful men of "culture" declare that the old-fashioned Gospel is unworthy of the nineteenth century with all its enlightenment, we are not surprised, for we knew that they would think so. Blind men are little pleased with color, and deaf men care little for music.

Human wisdom cannot make a man without eyes see the light. What do you know about the Gospel, oh you blinded wise men? What judges can you be of the light of revelation who seal up your eyes with the mud of your own cleverness, and then say you cannot see! Christ never intended that you should. He will only reveal Himself as He pleases, and He has pleased to do this to another kind of person from what you are. Oh, you that are wise in your own conceit, the gate of true wisdom is barred against you! You cannot by searching find out God, and when He graciously reveals Himself you refuse to see Him, and therefore it is just that you should perish in the dark. Well do you deserve this judgment. Let justice be done. That God had been pleased to reveal Himself to many through the preaching of the seventy was a great joy to Jesus. Let us also rejoice whenever God reveals Himself to men. Let us be glad when one who is simple in heart is made a child by divine grace through being born again. Let us furthermore rejoice whenever conversion is wrought by instruments that cannot possibly claim the glory of it. Let us praise and bless God that salvation is His own work from first to last. Come, all you who love the Father and say with the great Firstborn, "I thank thee, O Father, Lord of heaven and earth, that thou hast hid these things from the wise and prudent, and hast revealed them unto babes: even so, Father; for so it seemed good in thy sight."

Our Savior's Mode of Expressing That Joy

I have noticed some kind of joy in conversions which has not been wise in its expression, but has savored of glorying in the flesh. "Oh, we have had a wonderful time. We have had a blessed season! We have been visited by those dear men and have exerted ourselves in downright earnest to get up a revival. We have done wonders." Such talk will not do. Hear how the Savior speaks. His joy finds tongue in thanksgiving, "I thank thee, O Father." He ascribes the work to the Father, and then renders all the praise to Him. This is the eloquence of joy—"I thank thee, O Father." Friends, whenever you are happy, sing hymns of thanksgiving. "Is any merry? let him sing psalms" (James 5:13). The fittest language for joy, whether it be on earth or in heaven, is adoration and thanksgiving to God. Blessed be the name of the Lord that we are gladdened in the harvest field of Christian work, for it is He that gives seed to the sower and causes the Word to spring up and bring forth fruit a hundredfold.

Our Lord found expression for His joy in *declaring the Father's sovereignty*. "I thank thee, O Father, Lord of heaven and earth." Some shrink back from the idea of God as Lord of all things above and below. To them the free will of man seems the greatest of all facts. Lest there should be the slightest intrusion upon man's domain, they would have God limited as to His absolute power. To magnify man they would minimize God. You will hear them talking against those of us who magnify divine sovereignty, and imputing to us the notion of a certain arbitrariness in God, although such a thought has never entered our minds. Jehovah, who gives no account of His matters, but orders all things according to the good pleasure of His will, is never arbitrary, unjust, or tyrannical. Yet He is absolute and uncontrolled, a sovereign who reigns by His own self-existent power, Himself the source and origin of all law. He can be trusted with absolute sovereignty because He is infinite love and infinite goodness. I will go the utmost length as to the absolute supremacy of God, and His right to do as He wills, especially to do as He wills with His own, which Gospel grace most certainly is. He will have mercy on whom He will have mercy, and He will have compassion on whom He will have compassion. None can stay His hand or say to Him, What are you doing? When Christ was gladdest He expressed that gladness by ascribing to God an infinite sovereignty. Shall that truth be gloomy to us? No, rather we will each one view the work of the Father's grace and cry, "I thank You, O Father, and I thank You all the more because I know that You are Lord of heaven and earth."

If I am addressing any who quarrel with the doctrine of the sovereignty of God, I would advise them to cease their rebellion for "the Lord reigneth." Let them at least go as far as the Psalm, "Let the people tremble" (99:1). Even if they cannot go a little further and sing, "The Lord reigneth; let the earth rejoice; let the multitude of isles be glad thereof" (97:1). Power and rule are best in the hands of the great Jehovah who ever links together in His own single character both fatherhood and sovereignty. "I thank thee, O Father, Lord of heaven and earth." Dismiss from your minds all caricatures of the doctrine and receive it in its purest form—"the Lord is king for ever and ever. Hallelujah." Your joy, if it be deeply spiritual and very great, will never find room enough for the sweep of its Atlantic waves until you delight yourself in the absolute supremacy of God. The deep ground swell of delight within the Redeemer's soul could find no grander space over which it could expand its force than the unlimited power and dominion of the Lord of heaven and earth whose key it is that opens or shuts the kingdom of heaven, whose word it is that hides or reveals the things of eternity.

Our Lord *delighted in the special act of sovereignty* which was before Him, that the Lord had "hid these things from the wise and prudent, and had revealed them unto babes." He communed with God in it. He took pleasure in it and said, "Even so, Father; for so it seemed good in thy sight." His voice, as it were, went with the Father's voice. He agreed with the Father's choice, He rejoiced in it, He triumphed in it. The will of the Father was the will of Christ, and He had fellowship with the Father in every act of His sovereign choice. Yes, He magnified God for it in His inmost Spirit. He says, "Even so, Father; for so it seemed good in thy sight." He knew that what seems good to God must be good. Some things seem good to us which are evil, but that which seems good to God is good. Jesus praises God about it for no other reason than it is God's good pleasure that it should be so. Oh, what a state of heart it will be for you and me to get into when we can express our highest joy by a perfect acquiescence in the will of God, whatever that will may be. See here, beloved, the road to contentment, to peace, to happiness, yes, heavenly life this side of the grave. If you ever come to feel that what pleases God pleases you, you will be glad even in affliction and tribulation. If your heart is ever schooled down to accept as your will that which is God's will, and to believe anything to be good because God thinks it good, then you may go through the rest of your days singing and waiting until your Lord takes you to His own bosom. Soon will you rise to the place where all the singers meet and sing forever to God and the Lamb, all self and rebellion being forever banished. Herein, then, Christ found a channel for His joy—in thanksgiving, in magnifying the divine sovereignty, in having communion with it and in delighting in it.

Our Lord's Explanation of the Father's Act

The Father had been pleased to hide these things from the wise and prudent and to reveal them to babes. Jesus Christ is perfectly satisfied with that order of things, quite content with the kind of converts He has and the kind of preachers that God has given Him.

For, first, *the Lord Jesus does not need prestige*. Read the twenty-second verse—"All things are delivered to me of my Father." A mere pretender, when he begins to prophesy and set himself up for a religious leader, how pleased he is when some learned doctor endorses his claims! If some man of wealth and station comes to his side how he plumes himself. The Savior of our souls sought no such aids. The verdict of the world's *literati* could not make His word more truthful than it is, nor more convincing, for its power lies in the Spirit which reveals it. If great men say "Aye," they will not make His doctrine more sure; nor will they make it less truthful if they all say "Nay." Prestige for Christ! It is blasphemy to think of such a thing. "All things," says He, "are delivered to me of my Father." High priests and leaders of religion denounce Him, but all things are delivered to Him of His Father. The Sanhedrin determine to put Him down, but all things are delivered to Him of the Father. The learned deride His claims to be the Messiah! What matters it to Christ? The Father has committed all things into His hand. He stands alone and asks for no allies. His own power, unborrowed and unaided, is quite sufficient for His purposes. Do you think, friends, that we are going to stay our preaching of the Gospel until we shall have the so-called culture and intellect of the age upon our side to say, "It is even so"? Not we, but rather do we believe God in the teeth of the wiseacres and say, "Let God be true, but every man a liar" (Rom. 3:4). Jesus needs no imprimatur from scholars, no patronage from princes, no apologies from orators. The pomp and power and wisdom and cunning of the world were not with Him, and He thanks God that He is not encumbered with such doubtful gain. Instead He thanks God that this truth has been revealed to those who are not wise in their own eyes, nor intelligent in their own esteem, but, like children, willing to learn from God and glad to believe all that He reveals.

See how the Lord explains it yet further, by showing that *human wisdom cannot find out God*. "No man knoweth who the Son is but the

Father, and who the Father is but the Son." No man, though he be a master in Israel. Men of science may puzzle their brains, and with great ingenuity they may try to thread the intricacies of the unknown, but they must err from the truth if they refuse revelation. Such a thing as natural religion, spontaneously born of man's intellect, does not exist. "Oh," say you, "surely there is much of it." I say that whatever is truly religious in it was borrowed from revelation and has been handed down by tradition. Talk of comparative religions—there is but one, and the other pretenders have stolen certain of its clothes. Men see, no doubt, much of God in nature, but they would not have done so had there been no revelation. First came the light through revelation, and then afterward, when men saw it reflected from various objects, they dreamed that the light came out of the reflectors.

Men hear something of revealed truth. When their thoughts run in that line, that which they have heard is awakened in their minds. They then think themselves inventors. God is not known except as He reveals Himself, nor can He be discovered by human ingenuity. Carnal wit and thought tend not that way, but tend from God to blackest darkness. God is only to be known through Christ, so the text says: "No man knoweth who the Father is, but the Son, and he to whom the Son will reveal him." As the light, after God had created it was lodged in the sun, so is all knowledge of God treasured up in Christ as the Sun of righteousness. He it is that in Himself has light, the light that lightens every man that comes into the world, if he be lightened at all. We must receive Christ or abide in darkness. Yes, and the light that is in Christ is not perceptible by any man except by revelation. What says the text, "No man knoweth who the Son is, but the Father; and who the Father is, but the Son, and he to whom the Son will reveal him"? There must be a special and distinct revelation of Christ, and of the Father by Christ to each man, or else He will remain in blindness to the day of His death.

The power, then, which lies in merely human wisdom is a force which often hinders men from coming under the influence of revelation. Only by revelation can they know and by a revelation personally receive. But the man is so wise that he does not want to be taught, he can find it out for himself. Yield himself to an infallible book or an infallible spirit? Not he! Well, then, because of his very wisdom he becomes incapable of learning. Truth to tell, what is human wisdom? The supposed wisdom of man is folly, that is the short for it all. They write a history sometime of religious thought, and of the various phases through which Christianity has gone, and on this they ground remarks. But I should like somebody to write a truthful history of philosophy. The history of philosophy is a record of the insanities of mankind—a catalog of lunacies. You shall see one generation of philosophers busily engaged in refuting those that went before them, and doing it very well indeed. But what will the next generation do? Why refute this! The philosophies that were current one hundred years ago are all exploded now, and all the teachings of today, except such as are clear matters of fact, will be exploded before I go down to my grave, if I live to be gray headed. There is not a philosopher now living that can be sure but what there is some other fact to be discovered yet which will upset every hypothesis that he has sent forth into the world. Philosophers who conceitedly glory over believers in revelation are fools, for they know nothing with certainty, and absolute certainty appertains only to divine revelation.

In those who pretend to wisdom apart from God folly abounds. There is no light in them, nor in any man except that which comes from the Spirit of God. That wisdom which sets itself up apart from God is atheism, because God knows, and He says to man, "I will teach you. I will reveal Myself to you by My Son." But wisdom says, "We do not want to be taught. We know of ourselves." Then you are a rival to God! You pretend to be superior to God, since you are not willing to learn of Him, but will rather trust yourself. This folly and this atheism are the reasons why God hides His mind from the wise and the clever. They reject Him, and therefore He gives them over to a judicial blindness. Christ thanks Him that He does, for it is but justice that He should do so. When the Lord is pleased to give to any man a childlike spirit then is he on the road to knowledge.

This is true even in science itself. The secrets of nature will never be revealed to the man who believes that he already knows them. Nature herself does not teach the man who comes to her with prejudice. A man who thinks he knows beforehand sits down to study nature, and what does he generally discover? Well, he learnedly dreams of a universal solvent, or that the baser metals can be transmuted into gold, or that there is a perpetual motion. Those, you say, are things philosophers believed years ago. Yes, but their theories of today are just as stupid, and the science of today will be the jest of the next century. The greatest absurdities have been the pets of philosophy for hundreds of years. Why was it that men did not know better? Because they did not go to nature and ask her to teach them what was fact. They made an hypothesis, and then they went to nature to force her to prove it, as they do now. They start with a prejudgment of what they would like to be, and then take facts and twist them around into their system, and so they blind themselves by their own wisdom.

Well, if it be so in nature, and I am sure it is, it is certainly more so in grace. For when a man comes to the Word of God and says, "Now I know theology beforehand. I do not come here to find my creed in the Bible and learn it like a child, but I come to turn texts about and make them fit into my system"; well, he will blind himself and will be a fool. It is right he should be blinded, for has he not done that willfully which must of necessity lead to such an end?

Friends, simple teachableness is the first essential for the reception of a revelation from God. If you have it today, if you are seeking after truth, if you are crying after her, and if you are willing that God should reveal her to you, if you are anxious that He should reveal truth to you in Christ, you are the sort of person upon whom God in sovereignty looks with divine favor and to such as you are will He reveal Himself. What is wanted is faith, a childlike, receptive faith. He does not want faith in a pope, not faith in a man, not faith in an old established creed, but faith in God. Oh, my hearer, be willing to learn of Him, and you shall not be left uninstructed.

Now a lesson or two, and I have done. The first lesson to be learned is this. If great men, if eminent men, if so-called learned men, are not converted, do not be cast down about it—it is not likely they will be. In the next place, if many converts are obscure persons, persons without note or name, do not be at all disgusted with that fact. Who are you that you should be? Who are you that you should despise any upon whom God has looked in favor? Rather rejoice exceedingly with your Lord that God has chosen the despised, and you with them.

Next, learn that the sovereignty of God is always exercised in such a way that the pure in heart may always rejoice in it. God never did a sovereign act in which the loving Christ Himself could not rejoice. Be content, therefore, to leave everything in the hand of God that you do not understand. When His way is in the sea, be quite as glad as when His way is in the sanctuary. When His footsteps are not known, feel that they are quite as righteous and quite as holy as when you can perceive the path in which He moves.

The ultimate honor of the Gospel is secured to God alone, let that be our last lesson. When the wind up of all things shall come, there shall be no honor to any of us, nor would we desire it. But out of it all, out of the choice of each one, and out of the revelation made to each one will come up, multiplied into a thousand thunders, the voice as of Christ in His whole mystical body, "I thank thee, O Father." This shall be the song of heaven concerning the whole matter, as well concerning the lost as the saved. "I thank thee, O Father, Lord of heaven and earth." There shall be no cavils among the pure in heart, nor questions among the perfected spirits, but the whole family reviewing the whole of the Father's government, the hiding as well as the revealing, shall at the last say, Christ leading the utterance, "I thank thee, O Father, Lord of heaven and earth, that thou hast hid these things from the wise and prudent, and hast revealed them unto babes."

Brothers and sisters, let us learn our need of a personal revelation, let us seek it if we have not yet received it. With a childlike spirit, let us seek it in Christ, for He only can reveal the Father to us. When we have it let it be our joy that we see Him revealing it to others. Let this be our prayer that the God of Jacob would yet bring others to Christ, who shall rejoice in the light that has made glad our eyes. The Lord be with you. Amen.

5

Christ's Prayer for Peter

But I have prayed for thee, that thy faith fail not (Luke 22:32).

Satan has a deadly hatred toward all good men. They may rest assured that, somewhere or other, he will meet them on their way to the Celestial City. John Bunyan, in his immortal allegory, placed him in one particular spot and described him as Apollyon straddling across the road. There swearing by his infernal den that the pilgrim should go no further, but that there and then he would spill poor Christian's soul. But the encounter with Apollyon does not happen in the same place to all pilgrims. I have known some of them assailed by him most fiercely at the outset of their march to Zion. Their first days as Christians have been truly terrible to them by reason of the Satanic attacks they have had to endure. But, afterward, when the Devil has left them, angels have ministered to them, and they have had years of peace and joy. You remember that, in the case of our Savior, no sooner was He baptized than He was led of the Spirit into the wilderness to be tempted of the Devil. In like manner, there are those whose fiercest trials from the adversary come at the beginning of their public ministry.

Others meet with their greatest conflicts in middle life when, perhaps, they are too apt to think themselves secure against the assaults of Satan, and to fancy that their experience and their knowledge will suffice to preserve them against his wiles. I know some, like Martin Luther, in whose voyage of life the middle passage has been full of storm and tempest, and they have scarcely known what it was to have a moment's rest during all that period. Then there have been others, the first part of whose career has been singularly calm. Their life has been like a sea of glass, scarcely a ripple has been upon the waters. Yet, toward the end, the enemy has made up for it, and he has attacked them

This sermon was taken from *The Metropolitan Tabernacle Pulpit* and was preached on Sunday evening, January 22, 1882.

most ferociously right up to the last. I have known many instances of eminent saints who have had to die sword in hand, and enter heaven—I was about to say, with the marks of their stern conflict fresh upon them. At any rate, they have been crowned on the battlefield and have fallen asleep at the close of a tremendous fight.

With most of us who are really going to heaven—I will not say that it is a rule without any exception—but with most of us, at some time or another, we shall know the extreme value of this prayer, "Lead us not into temptation of any kind, but deliver us from *the evil one,* who, beyond all others, is especially to be dreaded." There is little to be gotten out of him, even if we conquer him. He usually leaves some mark of his prowess upon us, which we may carry to our graves. It were better to leap over hedge and ditch, and to go a thousand miles further on our pilgrim road than ever to have a conflict with him, except for those great purposes of which I shall presently speak a moment. The fight with Apollyon is a terrible ordeal—an ordeal, however, which a brave Christian will never think of shirking. No, rather will he rejoice that he has an enemy worthy of his steel, that true Damascus blade with which he is armed. In the name of God he will determine, though he wrestles not with flesh and blood, that he will contend against principalities and powers, and with the very leader of them all, that there may be all the more glory to the great King who makes the weakest of his followers to be so strong that they put the old dragon himself to flight.

So, dear friends, rest assured that Satan hates every good man. And that, some time or other, he is pretty sure to show that hatred in a very cruel and deadly attack upon him.

Further, because of his hatred, Satan earnestly desires to put believers into his sieve that he may sift them as wheat—not that he wants to get the chaff away from them, but simply that he may agitate them. You see the corn in the sieve, how it goes up and down, to and fro. There is not a single grain of it that is allowed to have a moment's rest. It is all in commotion and confusion, and the man who is sifting it takes care to sift first one way, and next another way, and then all sorts of ways. Now, that is just what Satan does with those whom he hates when he gets the opportunity. He sifts them in all manner of ways, and puts their whole being into agitation and turmoil. When he gets a hold of us, it is a shaking and sifting indeed. He takes care that anything like rest or breathing space shall be denied to us.

Satan desires thus to sift the saints in his sieve. At times, God grants his desire. If you look at the Revised Version, in the margin you learn the true idea of Satan having asked, or rather obtained by asking, the power to sift Peter as wheat. God sometimes gives Satan the permission to sift as wheat those who are undoubtedly His people, and then he tosses them to and fro indeed. That record in the Book of Job of Satan appearing before God is just repeated in this story of Peter. The Devil had obtained from God liberty to try and test poor boasting Peter. If Christ had not obtained of God in answer to His intercession the promise of the preservation of Peter, then had it gone ill indeed with the self-confident apostle. God grants to Satan permission to try His people in this way because He knows how He will overrule it to His own glory and their good.

There are certain graces which are never produced in Christians, to a high degree, except by severe temptation. "I noticed," said one, "in what a chastened spirit a certain minister preached when he had been the subject of a most painful temptation." There is a peculiar tenderness, without which one is not qualified to shepherdize Christ's sheep and to feed His lambs—a tenderness, without which one cannot strengthen his brethren, as Peter was afterward to do, a tenderness which does not usually come—at any rate, to such a man as Peter, except by his being put into the sieve, and tossed up and down by Satanic temptation.

Let that stand as the preface of my sermon, for I shall not have so much to say upon that as upon another point.

First, observe, in our text, *the grand point of Satan's attack*. We can see that from the place where Jesus puts the strongest line of defense: "I have prayed for thee, that thy faith fail not." The point of Satan's chief attack on a believer, then, is his faith. Observe, secondly, *the peculiar danger of faith:* "That thy faith fail not." That is the danger—not merely lest it should be slackened and weakened, but lest it should fail. And then observe, thirdly, *the believer's grand defense:* "I have prayed for thee, that thy faith fail not."

The Grand Point of Satan's Attack

When he assails a child of God, his main assault is upon his faith. I suppose that the reason is, first, *because faith is the vital point in the Christian.* We are engrafted into Christ by faith, and faith is the point of contact between the believing soul and the living Christ. If, therefore, Satan could manage to cut through the graft just there, then he would defeat the Savior's work most completely. Faith is the very heart of true godliness, for "the just shall live by faith" (Rom. 1:17; Gal. 3:11; Heb. 10:38). Take faith away, and you have torn the heart out of the gracious man. Hence, Satan, as far as he can, aims his fiery darts at a believer's faith. If he can only destroy faith, then he has destroyed the very life of the Christian. "Without faith it is impossible to please [God]" (Heb. 11:6). Therefore, if the Devil could but get our faith away from us, we should cease to be pleasing to God and should cease to be "accepted in the Beloved." Therefore, friends, look well to your faith. It is the very head and heart of your being as before God. The Lord grant that it may never fail you!

I suppose that Satan also attacks faith because it is the chief of all our graces. Love, under some aspects, is the choicest. But to lead the van in conflict, faith must come first. And there are some things which are ascribed solely and entirely to faith and are never ascribed to love. If any man were to speak of our being justified by love, it would grate upon the ears of the godly. If any were to talk of our being justified by repentance, those of us who know our Bible would be up in arms against such a perversion of the truth. But they may speak as long as they like of our "being justified by faith" (Rom. 5:1), for that is a quotation from the Scriptures. In the matter of justification, faith stands alone. It lays hold on Christ's sacrifice and His righteousness, and thereby the soul is justified. Faith, if I may so say, is the leader of the graces in the day of battle. Hence Satan says to his demoniacal archers, "Fight neither with small nor great, save only with the king of Israel" (1 Kings 22:31)—shoot at faith, kill it if possible. If faith is slain, where is love, where is hope, where is repentance, where is patience? If faith be conquered, then it is as when a standard-bearer faints. The victory is virtually won by the archenemy if he is able to conquer faith, for faith is the noble chieftain among the graces of a saint.

I suppose, again, that Satan makes a dead set upon the faith of the Christian *because it is the nourishing grace.* All the other graces within us derive strength from our faith. If faith be at a low ebb, love is sure to burn very feebly. If faith should begin to fail, then would hope grow dim. Where is courage? It is a poor puny thing when faith is weak. Take any grace you please, and you shall see that its flourishing depends upon the healthy condition of faith in our Lord Jesus Christ. To take faith away, therefore, would be to take the fountain away from the stream or to withdraw the sun from his rays of light. If you destroy the source, of course that which comes out of it thereupon ceases. Therefore, beloved, take the utmost possible care of your faith, for I may truly say of it that out of it are the issues of life to all your graces. Faith is that virtuous woman who clothes the whole household in scarlet, and feeds them all with luscious and strengthening food. But if faith be gone, the household soon becomes naked, poor, blind, and miserable. Everything in a Christian fails when faith ceases to nourish it.

Next to this, Satan attacks faith *because it is the great preserving grace.* The apostle says, "Above all"—that is, "over all," "covering all"—"taking the shield of faith, wherewith ye shall be able to quench all the fiery darts of the wicked." Sometimes, the Eastern soldiers had shields so large that they were like doors, and they covered the man from head to foot. Others of them, who used smaller shields, nevertheless handled them so deftly and moved them so rapidly, that it was tantamount to the shield covering the entire person. An arrow is aimed at the forehead, up goes the shield, and the sharp point rings on the metal. A javelin is hurled at the heart, but the shield turns it aside. The fierce foe aims a poisonous dart at the leg, but the shield intercepts it. Virtually, the shield is all-surrounding—so it is with your faith. As one has well said, "It is armor upon armor, for the helmet protects the head, but the shield protects both helmet and head. The breastplate guards the breast, but the buckler or shield defends the breastplate as well as the breast." Faith is a grace to protect the other graces. There is nothing like it. Therefore I do not wonder that Satan attacks faith when he sees its prominent position and its important influence in the entire town of Mansoul.

I cannot help saying, also, that I wonder not that Satan attacks faith *because it is the effective or efficient grace.* You know what a wonderful chapter that 11th chapter of the Epistle to the Hebrews is. It is a triumphal arch erected in honor of what? Of faith. According to that chapter, faith did everything. It quenched the fire, stopped the mouths of lions, turned to flight the armies of the aliens, received the dead who were raised, and so on. Faith is the soul's right hand. Faith works by love, but, still, it is faith that works. You can do nothing acceptably before God unless you do it by that right hand of faith. Hence, Satan cannot endure faith. He hates that most of all. Pharaoh tried to have all the male children thrown into the river because they were the fighting force of Israel. He did not mind having the women to grow up to bear burdens, it was the men whom he feared. And, in like manner, the Devil says, "I must stamp out faith, for that is the secret of strength." He will not trouble himself so much about your other graces, he will probably attack them when he can. But, first of all he says, "Down with faith! That is the man-child that must be destroyed." He aims his sharpest and deadliest darts at it.

I believe, also, that faith is attacked by Satan, most of all, *because it is most obnoxious to him.* He cannot endure faith. How do I know that? Why, because God loves it. If God loves faith, and if Christ crowns faith, I am sure that Satan hates it. What are we told concerning the work of Jesus being hindered by unbelief? "He did not many mighty works there because of their unbelief" (Matt. 13:58). Now, I will turn that text around and say of Satan that he cannot do many mighty works against some men because of their faith. Oh, how he sneaks off when he discovers a right royal faith in a man! He knows when he has met his master. He says, "Why should I waste my arrows upon a shield carried by such a man as that? He believes in God, he believes in Christ, he believes in the Holy Spirit. He is more than a match for me." To those that are under his leadership he cries, "To your tents!" He bids them flee away and escape, for he knows that there can be no victory for them when they come into collision with true God-given faith. He cannot bear to look at it. It blinds him. The lustrous splendor of that great shield of faith which shines as though a man did hang the sun upon his arm, and bear it before him into the fray, blinds even the mighty prince of darkness. Satan does but glance at it, and straightway he takes to flight, for he cannot endure it. He knows it is the thing which most of all helps to overthrow his kingdom and destroy his power. Therefore, believer, cling to your faith! Be like the young Spartan warrior, who would either bring his shield home with him or be brought home dead upon his shield. "Cast not away your confidence, which hath great recompence of reward." Whatever else you have not, "have faith in God" (Mark 11:22). Believe in the Christ of God. Rest your soul's entire confidence upon the faithful promise and the faithful Promiser. If you do so, Satan's attacks upon you will all be in vain.

That is my first point—observe the grand point of Satanic attack.

The Peculiar Danger of Faith

Did Peter's faith fail? Yes, and no. It failed in a measure, but it did not altogether fail. It failed in a measure, for he was human. But it did not altogether fail, for, at the back of it, there was the superhuman power which comes through the pleading of Christ. Poor Peter! He denied his Master, yet his faith did not utterly fail. I will show you why it did not. If you and I, beloved, are ever permitted to dishonor God and to deny our Lord as Peter did, yet may God in mercy keep us from the utter and entire failure of our faith as He kept Peter!

Notice, first, there was still some faith in Peter, even when he had denied his Master. When the Lord turned and looked upon him, *he went out and wept bitterly*. If there had not been the true faith in Peter still, the Master might have looked upon him long before a tear would have coursed down his cheeks. The Lord not only looked on Judas, but He gave him a sop with Him out of the dish. He even let the traitor put his lips to Him and kiss Him. But all that had no weight with Judas. The reason why Christ's look had such an effect on Peter was because there was some faith in Peter still. You may blow as long as ever you like at the cold coals, and you will get no fire. But I have sometimes seen a servant kneel down when there has been just a little flame left in the coal in a corner of the grate, and she has blown it tenderly and gently so as to revive it. "It is not quite out," she says. At last, there has been a good fire once again. May God grant that we may never come to that sad condition. But, if we do, may He of His grace grant that there may still be that blessed little faith left, that weak and feeble faith which, through the breathing upon it of the Spirit of God, shall yet be fanned into a flame!

We are sure that there was this faith still in Peter, *or else, what would he have done?* What did Judas do? Judas did two things. First, he went to a priest, or to priests, and confessed to them. Then he went out and hanged himself. The two things were strangely connected. Peter did neither. Yet, if he had not had faith, he might have done both. To publicly deny his Master three times, and to support his denial with oaths and curses even when that Master was close by, and in his greatest exigency, must have put Peter into most imminent peril. If there had not been within his heart faith that his Master could yet pardon and restore him, he might, in his despair have done precisely what the traitor Judas did. Or, if he had not gone to that extremity of guilt, he would have hidden himself away from the rest of the apostles. But, instead of doing so, we soon find him again with John—I do not wonder that he was with John. They were old companions. But, in addition to that, the beloved John had so often leaned his head on the Master's bosom that he had caught the sweet infection of his Savior's tenderness. Therefore, he was just the one with whom Peter would wish to associate. I think that if I had ever denied my Lord as Peter did, in that public way, I should have run away and hidden myself from all my former companions. But he did not, you see. He seemed to say to himself, "The Master, with His dear tender heart, can still forgive me and receive me." So he clings to the disciples, and especially to John. Aye, and notice that on the day of our Lord's resurrection Peter was the first disciple to enter the sepulcher. Though "the other disciple did outrun Peter" (John 20:4) and reached the grave first, "yet went he not in" (John 20:5) until Peter led the way. "The Lord is risen indeed, and hath appeared to Simon" (Luke 24:34) is a remarkable passage. Paul, writing concerning Christ's resurrection, says that "he was seen of Cephas" (1 Cor. 15:5), that is, Peter. There was some special manifestation of our blessed Master to Simon Peter, who was waiting for it and privileged to witness it. This showed that his faith was kept from failing through the Savior's prayers.

Now, beloved, I say no more about Peter, but I speak to you about your own faith. Are you greatly troubled? Then, I pray that your faith may not fail. It is shaken; it is severely tried; but God grant that it may not fail! Something whispers within your heart, "Give up all religion, it is not true." To that lie, answer, "'Get thee behind me, Satan' (Matt. 16:23); for the religion of Jesus Christ is eternally, assuredly, infallibly true." Cling to it, for it is your life. Or, perhaps, the fiend whispers, "It is true enough to others. But it is not meant for you, you are not one of the Lord's people." Well, if you cannot come to Christ as a saint, come to Him as a sinner. If you dare not come as a child to sit at His table, come as a dog to eat the crumbs that fall under it. Only do come and never give up your faith.

If the arch-fiend whispers again, "You have been a deceiver. Your profession is all a mistake or a lie," say to him, "Well, if it be so, there is still forgiveness in Christ for all who come to God by Him." Perhaps you are coming to the Savior for the first time. You mean to cast yourself upon the blood and merit of Jesus, even if you have never done so before. I pray for you, dear coming one. O gracious Savior, do not let Satan crush out the faith of even the weakest of Your people! Blessed Intercessor, plead for that poor trembler in whom faith is almost dying out! Great High Priest, intercede for him that his faith may not utterly fail him, and that he may still cling to You!

What is to become of us if we have not faith in Jesus? I know that there are some who seem to get on well without it—so may the dogs, so may the wild beasts. They get on well enough without the children's garments or the children's bread. But you and I cannot. The moment I am unbelieving, I am unhappy. It is not a vain thing for me to believe in Christ. It is my life, it is my strength, it is my joy. I am a lost man, and it were better for me that I had never been born unless I have the privilege of believing. Give up faith? Remember what Satan said concerning Job, "Skin for skin, yea, all that a man hath will he give for his life" (Job 2:4); our life is wrapped up in our faith in Christ. We cannot give it up, and we will not give it up. Come on, fiends of hell or mockers of earth, we will not give it up. We will hold it fast, for it is part of the very warp and woof of our being. We believe in God and in His Son, our Lord and Savior Jesus Christ. It is our great concern that our faith should be well guarded and protected, for we know the peculiar danger to which it is exposed when it is assailed by Satan.

The Believer's Great Preservative and Defense

What is the great protection of our faith? Our Savior's intercession. Prayer is always good, it is ever a blessed thing. But notice that great letter-word in the text, "*I* have prayed for thee." It is the intercession of Christ that preserves our faith, and there are three things about it which make it precious beyond all price. It is prevalent, prevenient, and pertinent. First, it is *prevalent,* for if Jesus pleads, He must prevail. It is *prevenient,* for before the temptation comes to Peter, He says, "I have prayed for you. Satan has but obtained, by his asking, the permission to tempt you; but I have already prayed for you."

And, then, it was *pertinent*—that is, to the point. Christ had prayed the best prayer possible: "that thy faith fail not." Peter would not have known that this was to be the chief point of attack by Satan. He might have thought that Satan would attack his love. The Lord seems to hint at his thought about that by saying to him afterward, "Simon, son of Jonas, lovest thou me?" But the Savior knew that the hottest part of the battle would rage around Fort Faith. Therefore He prayed that the fortress might be well garrisoned and never be captured by the enemy—and it was not.

Whenever I begin to talk to you about the intercession of Christ, I feel inclined to sit down and let you think and look up and listen until you hear that voice, matchless in its music, pleading, pleading, pleading, with the Father. It were much better for you to realize it than for me to describe it. It was a blessed thing to hear one's mother pray—by accident, as we say, to pass the door that was ajar and to hear mother pleading for her boy or her girl. It is a very touching thing to hear your child praying for her father, or your wife breathing out her warm desires for her beloved. I do not know anything more charming than to hear, now and then, a stray prayer that was never meant to be heard on earth, but only in heaven. I like such eavesdroppings. Oh, but listen! It is Jesus who is praying. He shows His wounds and pleads the merit of His great sacrifice. Wonder of wonders, He pleads for me and for you! Happy man, happy woman, to have our faith preserved by such a mighty preservative as this—the intercession of Christ!

I want you specially to notice that *this intercession is the pleading of One who,* in the text, *seems directly to oppose Himself to the great adversary:* "Satan hath obtained thee by asking, that he may sift thee as wheat; but I have obtained thee by asking" (so I will venture to paraphrase it), "that thy faith fail not." There stands Satan. You cannot see him and need not want to. But that grim monster who has made kings and princes tremble, who has plucked angels from their spheres of light, and who has hurled bright spirits down from heaven to hell stands there to assail you. You may well be afraid, for God Himself permits him to sift you. Ah! but there also stands the ever-blessed One before whom an angel, fallen or unfallen, is but a tiny spark compared with the sun. There He stands girt about the paps with the golden girdle of His faithfulness, robed in the fair white linen of His matchless righteousness, upon His head a crown of glory that far outshines all constellations of stars and suns. He opposes His divine pleading to the demoniacal asking of the fallen one. Are you afraid now? It does seem to me unspeakably blessed to see it written here, "Satan hath desired to have thee that he may sift thee as wheat." Then to see over the top of it this word, "but I have prayed for thee." Oh, blessed "but!" How it seems to cast the fallen angel back again into the bottomless pit, and to bind him with chains and set a seal upon his prison: "But I have prayed for thee." Tempt on, then, O Devil. Tempt at your worst, for there is no fear now when this glorious shield of gold, the intercession of the Savior, covers the entire person of the poor attacked one! "I have prayed for thee, that thy faith fail not."

And then my last word is this: *It is an intercession which is absolutely certain of success.* In fact, He who offers it anticipates its success and discounts it by giving this precept to His servant: "and when thou art converted"—sure pledge, then, that he will be converted, that he will be turned back, however far he wanders—when you are restored, "strengthen thy brethren." Then, for certain, he will be restored, or else the Savior would not have given him a precept which could only be available if a certain, unlikely contingency should occur. O you who are a true child of God, you may be drenched, but you shall never be drowned! O warrior of the Cross, your shield may be covered with fiery darts, thickly as the saplings of a young forest grow. But no dart shall ever reach your heart! You may be wounded in head and hand and foot, you mayest be a mass of scars, but your life is given you. To Christ are you given as a prey, and you shall come out even from between the jaws of death and shall overcome Satan by Christ's power. Only trust Christ; only trust Him. Cling to your faith, beloved; cling to your faith! I would like to get a hold of that young man who has lately been listening to skeptical teachers and to whisper in his ear, "Cling to your faith, young man, for in losing that, you will lose all."

And to you who, alas! have fallen into sin after having made a profession of religion, let me say that however far you have gone astray, still believe that Jesus is able to forgive you. Come back to Him and seek His pardon now. And you, my hoary-headed brother whose hair is whitening for heaven, are you sorely beset by all sorts of temptations? Well, give me your hand, for I, too, know what this warfare means. Let us believe in God, my brother. Let us both believe in God. Though He should break us down worse than ever, though He should set us up as a target and let the Devil shoot at us all the arrows from his quiver, let us still believe in God. Come to this pass to which my soul has come full often and to which Job came of old, "'Though he slay me, yet will I trust in him.' Whatever He does to me—if He shall never smile upon me again—I will still believe Him. I can do no other." I dare not doubt Him. I must confide in Him. Where is there any ground for confidence if it be not in the God that cannot lie and in the Christ of the everlasting covenant whom He has set forth to be the propitiation for human sin, and in the Holy Spirit whose work it is to take of the things of Christ and reveal them to us?

May the blessed Trinity save and keep us all, for our Lord Jesus Christ's sake! Amen.

6

Christ's Plea for Ignorant Sinners

Then said Jesus, Father, forgive them; for they know not what they do (Luke 23:34).

What tenderness we have here, what self-forgetfulness, what almighty love! Jesus did not say to those who crucified Him, "Begone!" One such word, and they must have all fled. When they came to take Him in the garden, they went backward and fell to the ground when He spoke but a short sentence. Now that He is on the cross, a single syllable would have made the whole company fall to the ground or flee away in fright.

Jesus says not a word in His own defense. When He prayed to His Father, He might justly have said, "Father, note what they do to thy beloved Son. Judge them for the wrong they do to Him who loves them, and who has done all He can for them." But there is no prayer against them in the words that Jesus utters. It was written of old by the prophet Isaiah, "He made intercession for the transgressors," and here it is fulfilled. He pleads for His murderers, "Father, forgive them."

He does not utter a single word of upbraiding. He does not say, "Why do you do this? Why pierce the hands that fed you? Why nail the feet that followed after you in mercy? Why mock the Man who loved to bless you?" No; not a word even of gentle upbraiding, much less of anything like a curse. "Father, forgive them." You notice, Jesus does not say, "I forgive them," but you may read that between the lines. He says that all the more because He does not say it in words. But He has laid aside His majesty and is fastened to the cross. Therefore He takes the humble position of a suppliant, rather than the more lofty place of one

---

This sermon was taken from *The Metropolitan Tabernacle Pulpit* and was preached on Sunday evening, October 5, 1890.

67

who had power to forgive. How often when men say, "I forgive you," is there a kind of selfishness about it! At any rate, self is asserted in the very act of forgiving. Jesus takes the place of a pleader, a pleader for those who were committing murder upon Himself. Blessed be His name!

This word of the cross we shall use tonight. We shall see if we cannot gather something from it for our instruction. For though we were not there and did not actually put Jesus to death, yet we really caused His death. We, too, crucified the Lord of glory. His prayer for us was, "Father, forgive them; for they know not what they do."

I am not going to handle this text so much by way of exposition as by way of experience. I believe there are many here to whom these words will be very appropriate. This will be our line of thought. First, *we were in measure ignorant.* Secondly, *we confess that this ignorance is no excuse.* Thirdly, *we bless our Lord for pleading for us.* Fourthly, *we now rejoice in the pardon we have obtained.* May the Holy Spirit graciously help us in our meditation!

We Were in Measure Ignorant

We who have been forgiven, we who have been washed in the blood of the Lamb, we once sinned in a great measure through ignorance. Jesus says, "They know not what they do." Now, I shall appeal to you, brothers and sisters, when you lived under the dominion of Satan, and served yourselves and sin, was there not a measure of ignorance in it? You can truly say, as we said in the hymn we sang just now—

"Alas! I knew not what I did."

It is true, first, that we were ignorant of *the awful meaning of sin.* We began to sin as children. We knew that it was wrong, but we did not know all that sin meant. We went on to sin as young men; peradventure we plunged into much wickedness. We knew it was wrong, but we did not see the end from the beginning. It did not appear to us as rebellion against God. We did not think that we were presumptuously defying God, setting at nothing His wisdom, defying His power, deriding His love, spurning His holiness. Yet we were doing all that. There is an abysmal depth in sin. You cannot see to the bottom of it. When we rolled sin under our tongue as a sweet morsel, we did not know all the terrible ingredients compounded in that deadly bittersweet. We were in a measure ignorant of the tremendous crime we committed when we dared to live in rebellion against God. So far, I think, you go with me.

We did not know, at that time, God's *great love to us.* I did not know that He had chosen me from before the foundation of the world. I never dreamed of that. I did not know that Christ stood for me as my

Substitute to redeem me from among men. I did not know that He had espoused me to Himself in righteousness and in faithfulness to be one with Him forever. You, dear friends, who now know the love of Christ, did not understand it then. You did not know that you were sinning against eternal love, against infinite compassion, against a distinguishing love such as God had fixed on you from eternity. So far, we knew not what we did.

I think, too, that we did not know all that we were doing in our rejection of Christ and putting Him to grief. He came to us in our youth. Impressed by a sermon we began to tremble and to seek His face, but we were decoyed back to the world and refused Christ. Our mother's tears, our father's prayers, our teacher's admonitions often moved us, but we were very stubborn and rejected Christ. We did not know that in that rejection we were virtually putting Him away and crucifying Him. We were denying His Godhead, or else we should have worshiped Him. We were denying His love, or else we should have yielded to Him. We were practically, in every act of sin, taking the hammer and the nails, and fastening Christ to the cross; but we did not know it. Perhaps, if we had known it, we should not have crucified the Lord of glory. We did know we were doing wrong, but we did not know all the wrong that we were doing.

Nor did we know fully *the meaning of our delays*. We hesitated, we were on the verge of conversion, we went back and turned again to our old follies. We were hardened, Christless, prayerless still. Each one of us said, "Oh, I am only waiting a little while until I have fulfilled my present engagements, until I am a little older, until I have seen a little more of the world!" The fact is, we were refusing Christ and choosing the pleasures of sin instead of Him. Every hour of delay was an hour of crucifying Christ, grieving His Spirit, and choosing this harlot world in the place of the lovely and ever-blessed Christ. We did not know that.

I think we may add one thing more. *We did not know the meaning of our self-righteousness*. We used to think, some of us, that we had a righteousness of our own. We had been to church regularly, or we had been to the meeting house whenever it was open. We were christened; we were confirmed; or, peradventure, we rejoiced that we never had either of those things done to us. Thus, we put our confidence in ceremonies, or the absence of ceremonies. We said our prayers; we read a chapter in the Bible night and morning. We did—oh, I do not know what we did not do! But there we rested. We were righteous in our own esteem. We had not any particular sin to confess, nor any reason to lie in the dust before the throne of God's majesty. We were about as good as we could be. We did not know that we were even then perpetrating the highest insult upon Christ. For, if we were not sinners, why did

Christ die. If we had a righteousness of our own which was good enough, why did Christ come here to work out a righteousness for us? We made out Christ to be a superfluity by considering that we were good enough without resting in His atoning sacrifice. Ah, we did not think we were doing that! We thought we were pleasing God by our religiousness, by our outward performances, by our ecclesiastical correctness. But all the while we were setting up anti-Christ in the place of Christ. We were making out that Christ was not wanted. We were robbing Him of His office and glory! Alas! Christ could say of us, with regard to all these things, "They know not what they do." I want you to look quietly at the time past wherein you served sin, and just see whether there was not a darkness upon your mind, a blindness in your spirit, so that you did not know what you did.

We Confess That This Ignorance Is No Excuse

Our Lord might urge it as a plea, but we never could. We did not know what we did, and so we were not guilty to the fullest possible extent. But we were guilty enough, therefore let us own it.

For first, remember, *the law never allows this as a plea.* In our own English law, a man is supposed to know what the law is. If he breaks it, it is no excuse to plead that he did not know it. It may be regarded by a judge as some extenuation, but the law allows nothing of the kind. God gives us the law, and we are bound to keep it. If I erred through not knowing the law, still it was a sin. Under the Mosaic law there were sins of ignorance, and for these there were special offerings. The ignorance did not blot out the sin. That is clear in my text. For, if ignorance rendered an action no longer sinful, then why should Christ say, "Father, forgive them"? But He does. He asks for mercy for what is sin, even though the ignorance in some measure be supposed to mitigate the criminality of it.

But, dear friends, we might have known. If we did not know, it was because we would not know. There was the preaching of the Word, but we did not care to hear it. There was this blessed Book, but we did not care to read it. If you and I had sat down and looked at our conduct by the light of Holy Scripture, we might have known much more of the evil of sin, and much more of the love of Christ, and much more of the ingratitude which is possible in refusing Christ and not coming to Him.

In addition to that, we did not think. "Oh, but," you say, "young people never do think!" But young people should think. If there is anybody who need not think, it is the old man whose day is nearly over. If he does think, he has but a very short time in which to improve; but the young have all their life before them. If I were a carpenter and had to make a box, I should not think about it after I had made the box. I should think before I began to cut my timber what sort of box it was to be. In every action, a man thinks before he begins or else he is a fool. A young man ought to think more than anybody else, for now he is, as it were, making his box. He is beginning his life-plan. He should be the most thoughtful of all men. Many of us who are now Christ's people would have known much more about our Lord if we had given Him more careful consideration in our earlier days. A man will consider about taking a wife, he will consider about taking a business, he will consider about buying a horse or a cow; but he will not consider about the claims of Christ and the claims of the Most High God. This renders his ignorance willful and inexcusable.

Beside that, dear friends, although we have confessed to ignorance, *in many sins we did know a great deal.* Come, let me quicken your memories. There were times when you knew that such an action was wrong, when you started back from it. You looked at the gain it would bring you. You sold your soul for that price and deliberately did what you were well aware was wrong. Are there not some here saved by Christ who must confess that, at times, they did violence to their conscience? They did despite to the Spirit of God, quenched the light of heaven, drove the Spirit away from them distinctly knowing what they were doing. Let us bow before God in the silence of our hearts and own to all this. We hear the Master say, "Father, forgive them; for they know not what they do." Let us add our own tears as we say, "And forgive us, also, because in some things we did know, and in all things we might have known. But we were ignorant for want of thought, which thought was a solemn duty that we ought to have rendered to God."

One thing more I will say on this head. When a man is ignorant and does not know what he ought to do, what should he do? Well, he should do nothing until he does know. But here is the mischief of it, that *when we did not know, yet we chose to do the wrong thing.* If we did not know, why did we not choose the right thing? But, being in the dark, we never turned to the right, but always blundered to the left from sin to sin. Does not this show us how depraved our hearts are? Though we are seeking to be right, when we are let alone, we go wrong of ourselves. Leave a child alone, leave a man alone, leave a tribe alone without teaching and instruction, what comes of it? Why, the same as when you leave a field alone. It never, by any chance, produces wheat or barley. Leave it alone, and there are rank weeds, thorns, and briars showing that the natural set of the soil is toward producing that which is worthless. O friends, confess the innate evil of your hearts as well as the evil of your lives, in that, when you did not know, yet, having a perverse instinct, you chose the evil and refused the good. When you did not know enough of Christ and did not think enough of Him to know whether you ought to have Him or not, you would not come to Him that you might have life. You needed light, but you shut your eyes to the sun. You were thirsty, but you would not drink of the living spring. So your ignorance, though it was there, was a criminal ignorance which you must confess before the Lord. Oh, come to the cross, you who have been there before and have lost your burden there! Come and confess your guilt over again and clasp that cross afresh. Look to Him who bled upon it and praise His dear name that He once prayed for you, "Father, forgive them; for they know not what they do."

Now, I am going a step further. We were in a measure ignorant, but we confess that that measurable ignorance was no excuse.

We Bless Our Lord for Pleading for Us

Do you notice when it was that Jesus pleaded? It was *while they were crucifying Him.* They had just driven in the nails. They had lifted up the cross and dashed it down into its socket, dislocating all his bones, so that he could say, "I am poured out like water, and all my bones are out of joint" (Ps. 22:14). Ah, dear friends, it was then that, instead of a cry or a groan, this dear Son of God said, "Father, forgive them; for they know not what they do." They did not ask forgiveness for themselves; Jesus asked forgiveness for them. Their hands were imbrued in His blood. It was then, even then, that He prayed for them. Let us think of the great love wherewith He loved us, even while we were yet sinners, when we rioted in sin, when we drank it down as the ox drinks down water. Even then He prayed for us. "When we were yet without strength, in due time Christ died for the ungodly" (Rom. 5:6). Bless His name tonight. He prayed for you when you did not pray for yourself. He prayed for you when you were crucifying Him.

Then think of His plea. *He pleads His Sonship.* He says, *"Father,* forgive them." He was the Son of God, and He puts His divine Sonship into the scale on our behalf. He seems to say, "Father, as I am Your Son, grant Me this request and pardon these rebels. Father, forgive them." The filial rights of Christ were very great. He was the Son of God, not as we are by adoption, but by nature. By eternal filiation He was the Son of the Highest, "Light of light, very God of very God," the second Person in the Divine Trinity. He puts that Sonship here before God and says, "Father, Father, forgive them." Oh, the power of that word from the Son's lips when He is wounded, when He is in agony, when He is dying! He says, "Father, Father, grant My one request. 'O Father, forgive them; for they know not what they do.'" The great Father bows His awful head in token that the petition is granted.

Then notice that Jesus here silently, but really, *pleads His sufferings.* The attitude of Christ when He prayed this prayer is very noteworthy.

His hands were stretched upon the transverse beam; His feet were fastened to the upright tree; there He pleaded. Silently His hands and feet were pleading, and His agonized body from every sinew and muscle pleaded with God. His sacrifice was presented there before the Father's face; not yet complete, but in His will complete. So it is His cross that takes up the plea, "Father, forgive them." O blessed Christ! It is thus that we have been forgiven, for His Sonship and His cross have pleaded with God and have prevailed on our behalf.

I love this prayer, also, because of the *indistinctness* of it. It is "Father, forgive them." He does not say, "Father, forgive the soldiers who have nailed me here." He includes them. Neither does He say, "Father, forgive the people who are beholding Me." He means them. Neither does He say, "Father, forgive sinners in ages to come who will sin against Me." But He means them. Jesus does not mention them by any accusing name: "Father, forgive My enemies. Father, forgive My murderers." No, there is no word of accusation upon those dear lips. "Father, forgive them." Now into that pronoun "them" I feel that I can crawl. Can you get in there? Oh, by a humble faith, appropriate the cross of Christ by trusting in it, and get into that big, little word "them"! It seems like a chariot of mercy that has come down to earth into which a man may step, and it shall bear him up to heaven. "Father, forgive them."

Notice, also, what it was that Jesus asked for. To omit that would be to leave out the very essence of His prayer. *He asked for full absolution for His enemies:* "Father, forgive them. Do not punish them; forgive them. Do not remember their sin; forgive it. Blot it out and throw it into the depths of the sea. Remember it not, My Father. Mention it not against them any more forever. Father, forgive them." Oh, blessed prayer, for the forgiveness of God is broad and deep! When man forgives, he leaves the remembrance of the wrong behind. But when God pardons, He says, "I will forgive their iniquity, and I will remember their sin no more" (Jer. 31:34). It is this that Christ asked for you and me long before we had any repentance or any faith. In answer to that prayer, we were brought to feel our sin, brought to confess it, and to believe in Him. Now, glory be to His name, we can bless Him for having pleaded for us and obtained the forgiveness of all our sins.

We Now Rejoice in the Pardon We Have Obtained

Have you obtained pardon? Is this your song?

> Now, oh joy! my sins are pardon'd,
> Now I can, and do believe.

I have a letter in my pocket from a man of education and standing who has been an agnostic. He says that he was a sarcastic agnostic. He writes praising God and invoking every blessing upon my head for bringing him to the Savior's feet. He says, "I was without happiness for this life, and without hope for the next." I believe that that is a truthful description of many an unbeliever. What hope is there for the world to come apart from the cross of Christ? The best hope such a man has is that he may die the death of a dog, and there may be an end of him. What is the hope of the Romanist when he comes to die? I feel so sorry for many devout and earnest friends, for I do not know what their hope is. They do not hope to go to heaven yet, at any rate. Some purgatorial pains must be endured first. All, this is a poor, poor faith to die on to have such a hope as that to trouble your last thoughts. I do not know of any religion but that of Christ Jesus which tells us of sin pardoned, absolutely pardoned. Now, listen. Our teaching is not that when you come to die you may, perhaps, find out that it is all right, but "Beloved, now are we the sons of God" (1 John 3:2). "He that believeth on the Son hath everlasting life" (John 3:36). He has it now, knows it, and rejoices in it. So I come back to the last head of my discourse, we rejoice in the pardon Christ has obtained for us. We are pardoned. I hope that the larger portion of this audience can say, "By the grace of God, we know that we are washed in the blood of the Lamb."

Pardon has come to us through Christ's plea. Our hope lies in the plea of Christ, and specially in His death. If Jesus paid my debt, and He did if I am a believer in Him, then I am out of debt. If Jesus bore the penalty of my sin, and He did if I am a believer, then there is no penalty for me to pay, for we can say to Him—

> Complete atonement thou hast made,
> And to the utmost farthing paid
>   Whate'er thy people owed:
> Nor can his wrath on me take place,
> If shelter'd in thy righteousness,
>   And sprinkled with thy blood.
>
> If thou hast my discharge procured,
> And freely in my room endured
>   The whole of wrath divine:
> Payment God cannot twice demand,
> First at my bleeding Surety's hand,
>   And then again at mine.

If Christ has borne no punishment, I shall never bear it. Oh, what joy there is in this blessed assurance! Your hope that you are pardoned lies in this, that Jesus died. Those dear wounds of His bleed life for you.

We praise Him for our pardon because *we do know now what we did*. Oh, friends, I know not how much we ought to love Christ because we sinned against Him so grievously! Now we know that sin is "exceeding sinful" (Rom. 7:13). Now we know that sin crucified Christ. Now we know that we stabbed our heavenly Lover to His heart. We slew, with ignominious death, our best and dearest Friend and Benefactor. We know that now. We could almost weep tears of blood to think that we ever treated Him as we did. But it is all forgiven, all gone. Oh, let us bless that dear Son of God who has put away even such sins as ours! We feel them more now than ever before. We know they are forgiven, and our grief is because of the pain that the purchase of our forgiveness cost our Savior. We never knew what our sins really were until we saw Him in a bloody sweat. We never knew the crimson hue of our sins until we read our pardon written in crimson lines with His precious blood. Now, we see our sin, and yet we do not see it. God has pardoned it, blotted it out, cast it behind His back forever.

Henceforth *ignorance,* such as we have described, *shall be hateful to us*. Ignorance of Christ and eternal things shall be hateful to us. If, through ignorance, we have sinned, we will have done with that ignorance. We will be students of His Word. We will study that masterpiece of all the sciences, the knowledge of Christ crucified. We will ask the Holy Spirit to drive far from us the ignorance that engenders sin. God grant that we may not fall into sins of ignorance any more. But may we be able to say, "I know whom I have believed. Henceforth I will seek more knowledge until I comprehend, with all saints, what are the heights, depths, lengths, and breadths of the love of Christ, and know the love of God which passes knowledge"!

I put in a practical word here. If you rejoice that you are pardoned, *show your gratitude by your imitation of Christ*. There was never before such a plea as this, "Father, forgive them; for they know not what they do." Plead like that for others. Has anybody been injuring you? Are there persons who slander you? Pray tonight, "Father, forgive them; for they know not what they do." Let us always render good for evil, blessing for cursing. When we are called to suffer through the wrongdoing of others, let us believe that they would not act as they do if it were not because of their ignorance. Let us pray for them and make their very ignorance the plea for their forgiveness: "Father, forgive them; for they know not what they do."

I want you also to think of the millions of London just now. See those miles of streets pouring out their children this evening or look at those public houses with the crowds streaming in and out. Go down our streets by moonlight. See what I almost blush to tell. Follow men and women, too, to their homes, and be this your prayer: "Father, forgive them; for they know not what they do." That silver bell—keep it always ringing. What did I say? That silver bell? No, it is the *golden* bell upon the priest's garments. Wear it on your garments, you priests of God, and let it always ring out its golden note, "Father, forgive them; for they know not what they do." If I can set all God's saints imitating Christ with such a prayer as this, I shall not have spoken in vain.

Friends, I see *reason for hope in the very ignorance that surrounds us*. I see hope for this poor city of ours, hope for this poor country, hope for Africa, China, and India. "They know not what they do." Here is a strong argument in their favor, for they are more ignorant than we were. They know less of the evil of sin and less of the hope of eternal life than we do. Send up this petition, people of God! Heap your prayers together with cumulative power. Send up this fiery shaft of prayer straight to the heart of God while Jesus from His throne shall add His prevalent intercession, "Father, forgive them; for they know not what they do."

If there be any unconverted people here, and I know that there are some, we will mention them in our private devotion as well as in the public assembly. We will pray for them in words like these, "Father, forgive them; for they know not what they do." May God bless you all, for Jesus Christ's sake! Amen.

7

Christ's Pastoral Prayer for His People

I pray for them: I pray not for the world, but for them which thou hast given me; for they are thine. And all mine are thine, and thine are mine; and I am glorified in them (John 17:9–10).

To begin with, I remark that our Lord Jesus pleads for His own people. When He puts on His priestly breastplate, it is for the tribes whose names are there. When He presents the atoning sacrifice, it is for Israel whom God has chosen. He utters this great truth which some regard as narrow, but which we adore, "I pray for them: I pray not for the world." The point to which I want to call attention is this, the reason why Christ prays not for the world, but for His people. He puts it, "For they are thine," as if they were all the dearer to Him because they were the Father's: "I pray for them: I pray not for the world, but for them which thou hast given me, for they are thine." We might have half thought that Jesus would have said, "They are Mine, and therefore I pray for them." It would have been true, but there would not have been the beauty of truth about it which we have here. He loves us all the better, and He prays for us all the more fervently, because we are the Father's. Such is His love to His Father that our being the Father's sheds upon us an extra halo of beauty. Because we belong to the Father, therefore does the Savior plead for us with all the greater earnestness at the throne of the heavenly grace.

But this leads us on to remember that our Lord had undertaken suretyship engagements on account of His people. He undertook to preserve the Father's gift: "Those that thou gavest me I have kept, and none of them is lost." He looked upon the sheep of His pasture as belonging to

---

This sermon was taken from *The Metropolitan Tabernacle Pulpit* and was preached on Sunday evening, September 1, 1889.

77

His Father, and the Father had put them into His charge, saying to Him, "Of thine hand will I require them." As Jacob kept his uncle's flocks, by day the heat devoured him, and at night the frost. But he was more careful over them because they were Laban's than if they had been his own. He was to give an account of all the sheep committed to him, and he did so. He lost none of Laban's sheep. But his care over them was partly accounted for by the fact that they did not belong to himself, but belonged to his uncle Laban.

Understand this twofold reason, then, for Christ's pastoral prayer for His people. He first prays for them because they belong to the Father, and therefore have a peculiar value in His eye. Next, because they belong to the Father, He is under suretyship engagements to deliver them all to the Father in that last great day when the sheep shall pass under the rod of Him that tells them. Now you see where I am bringing you tonight. I am not going to preach at this time to the world any more than Christ upon this occasion prayed for the world. But I am going to preach to His own people as He in this intercessory prayer pleaded for them. I trust that they will all follow me, step by step, through this great theme. I pray the Lord that in these deep central truths of the Gospel we may find real refreshment for our souls tonight.

The Intensity of the Sense of Property That Christ Has in His People

Here are *six words setting forth Christ's property in those who are sacred:* "Them which thou hast *given me*"—(that is one); "for they are *thine. And all *mine* are *thine,* and *thine* are *mine; and I am glorified in them.*" There are certain persons so precious to Christ that they are marked all over with special tokens that they belong to Him. As I have known a man to write his name in a book which he has greatly valued. Then he has turned over some pages and has written his name again. As we have sometimes known persons, when they have highly valued a thing, to put their mark, their seal, their stamp, here, there, and almost everywhere upon it. So, notice in my text how the Lord seems to have the seal in His hand, and He stamps it all over His peculiar possession: "They are thine. And all mine are thine, and thine are mine." It is all possessive pronouns to show that God looks upon His people as His portion, His possession, His property. "They shall be mine, saith the LORD of hosts, in that day when I make up my jewels" (Mal. 3:17). Every man has something or other which he values above the rest of his estate. Here the Lord, by so often reiterating the words which signify possession, proves that He values His people above everything. Let us show that we appreciate this privilege of being set apart to God. Let us each one say to Him—

> Take my poor heart, and let it be
> For ever closed to all but thee!
> Seal thou my breast, and let me wear
> That pledge of love for ever there.

I call your attention, next, to the fact that while there are these six expressions here, *they are all applied to the Lord's own people.* "Mine" (that is, the saints) "are thine" (that is, the saints); "and thine" (that is, the saints) "are mine" (that is, the saints). These broad arrows of the King of kings are all stamped upon His people. While the marks of possession are numerous, they are all set upon one object. What, does not God care for anything else? I answer, No. As compared with His own people, He cares for nothing else. "The LORD's portion is his people; Jacob is the lot of his inheritance" (Deut. 32:9). Has not God other things? Ah, what is there that He has not? The silver and the gold are His, and the cattle on a thousand hills. All things are of God. Of Him and by Him and through Him and to Him are all things. Yet He reckons them not in comparison with His people. You know how you, dearly beloved, value your children much more than you do anything else. If there were a fire in your house tonight, and you could only carry one thing out of it, mother, would you hesitate a moment as to what that one thing should be? You would carry your babe, and let everything else be consumed in the flames. It is so with God. He cares for His people beyond everything else. He is the Lord God of Israel, and in Israel He has set His name, and there He takes His delight. There does He rest in His love, and over her does He rejoice with singing.

I want you to notice these different points, not because I can fully explain them all to you. But if I can only give you some of these great truths to think about and to help you to communion with Christ, I shall have done well. I want you to remark yet further concerning these notes of possession that *they occur in the private relationship between the Father and the Son.* It is in our Lord's prayer when He is in the inner sanctuary speaking with the Father that we have these words, "All mine are thine, and thine are mine." It is not to you and to me that He is talking now. The Son of God is speaking with the Father when they are in very near communion one with the other. Now, what does this say to me but that the Father and the Son greatly value believers? What people talk about when they are alone, not what they say in the market, not what they talk of in the midst of the confused mob, but what they say when they are in private that lays bare their heart. Here is the Son speaking to the Father, not about thrones and royalties, nor cherubim and seraphim, but about poor men and women, in those days mostly fishermen and peasant folk, who believed on Him. They are talking about these people, and the Son is taking His own solace with the Father in their secret privacy by talking about these precious jewels, these dear ones that are Their peculiar treasure.

You have not any notion how much God loves you. Dear brother, dear sister, you have never yet had half an idea, in the tithe of an idea, of how precious you are to Christ. You think because you are so imperfect and fall so much below your own ideal that, therefore, He does not love you much. You think that He cannot do so. Have you ever measured the depth of Christ's agony in Gethsemane and of His death on Calvary? If you have tried to do so, you will be quite sure that apart from anything in you or about you, He loves you with a love that passes knowledge. Believe it. "But I do not love Him as I should," I think I hear you say. No, and you never will unless you first know His love to you. Believe it—believe it to the highest degree—that He so loves you that when there is no one who can commune with Him but the Father, even then their converse is about their mutual estimate of you, how much they love you: "All mine are thine, thine are mine."

Only one other thought under this head. I do but put it before you and leave it with you, for I cannot expound it tonight. *All that Jesus says is about all His people,* for He says, "All mine are thine, and thine are mine." These high, secret talks are not about some few saints who have reached a "higher life," but about all of us who belong to Him. Jesus bears all of us on His heart, and He speaks of us all to the Father: "All mine are thine." "That poor woman who could never serve her Lord except by patient endurance, she is Mine," says Jesus. "She is Thine, great Father." "That poor girl, newly converted, whose only spiritual life was spent upon a sickbed, and then she exhaled to heaven like a dewdrop of the morning, she is Mine, and she is Thine. That poor child of Mine who often stumbles, who never brought much credit to the sacred name, he is Mine, and he is Thine. All Mine are Thine." I seem as if I heard a silver bell ringing out. The very tones of the words are like the music from the harps of angels: "Mine—Thine; Thine—Mine." May such sweet risings and fallings of heavenly melodies charm all our ears!

I think that I have said enough to show you the intensity of the sense of property which Christ has in His people: "All mine are thine, and thine are mine."

The Intensity of United Interest Between the Father and the Son Concerning Believers

First, let me say that *Jesus loves us because we belong to the Father.* Turn that truth over. "My Father has chosen them. My Father loves them. Therefore," says Jesus, "I love them and lay down My life for them. I will take My life again for them and live throughout eternity for them. They are dear to Me because they are dear to My Father." Have you not often loved another person for the sake of a third one upon whom all your heart was set? There is an old proverb, and I cannot help quoting it just now. It is, "Love me, love my dog." It is as if the Lord Jesus so loved the Father that even such poor dogs as we are get loved by Him for His Father's sake. To the eyes of Jesus we are radiant with beauty because God has loved us.

Now turn that thought around the other way, *the Father loves us because we belong to Christ*. At first, the Father's love in election was sovereign and self-contained. But now, today, since He has given us over to Christ, He takes a still greater delight in us. "They are My Son's sheep," says He. "He bought them with His blood." Better still, "That is My Son's spouse," says He. "That is My Son's bride. I love her for His sake." There was that first love which came fresh from the Father's heart, but now, through this one channel of love to Jesus, the Father pours a double flood of love on us for His dear Son's sake. He sees the blood of Jesus sprinkled on us. He remembers the token, and for the sake of His beloved Son He prizes us beyond all price. Jesus loves us because we belong to the Father, and the Father loves us because we belong to Jesus.

Now come closer still to the central thought of the text, "All mine are thine." *All who are the Son's are the Father's*. Do we belong to Jesus? Then we belong to the Father. Have I been washed in the precious blood? Can I sing tonight—

> The dying thief rejoiced to see
> That fountain in his day;
> And there have I, though vile as he,
> Washed all my sins away?

Then, by redemption I belong to Christ but at the same time I may be sure that I belong to the Father: "All mine are thine." Are you trusting in Christ? Then you are one of God's elect. That high and deep mystery of predestination need trouble no man's heart if he be a believer in Christ. If you believe in Christ, Christ has redeemed you, and the Father chose you from before the foundation of the world. Rest happy in that firm belief, "All mine are thine." How often have I met with people puzzling themselves about election! They want to know if they are elect. No man can come to the Father but by Christ; no man can come to election except through redemption. If you have come to Christ and are His redeemed, it is certain beyond all doubt that you were chosen of God and are the Father's elect. "All mine are thine."

So, if I am bought by Christ's precious blood, I am not to sit down and say how grateful I am to Christ as though He were apart from the Father, and more loving and more tender than the Father. No, no; I belong to the Father if I belong to Christ. I have for the Father the same gratitude, the same love, and I would render the same service as to Jesus, for Jesus puts it, "All mine are thine."

If, also, I am a servant of Christ, if, because He bought me I try to serve Him, then I am a servant of the Father if I am a servant of the Son. "All Mine, whatever position they occupy, belong to You, great Father." They have all the privileges which come to those who belong to the Father. I hope that I do not weary you. I cannot make these things entertaining to the careless. I do not try to do so. But you who love my Lord and His truth ought to rejoice to think that, in being the property of Christ, you are assured that you are the property of the Father. "All mine are thine."

> With Christ our Lord we share our part
> In the affections of his heart;
> Nor shall our souls be thence removed
> Until he forgets his first-beloved.

But now you have to look at the other part of it: "and thine are mine." *All who are the Father's are the Son's.* If you belong to the Father, you belong to the Son. If you are elect, and so the Father's, you are redeemed, and so the Son's. If you are adopted, and so the Father's, you are justified in Christ, and so you are the Son's. If you are regenerated, and so are begotten of the Father, yet still your life is dependent upon the Son. Remember that while one biblical figure sets us forth as children who have each one a life within himself, another equally valid figure represents us as branches of the Vine which die unless they continue united to the stem. "All thine are mine." If you are the Father's, you must be Christ's. If your life is given you of the Father, it still depends entirely upon the Son.

What a wonderful mixture all this is! The Father and the Son are one, and we are one with the Father and with the Son. A mystic union is established between us and the Father by reason of our union with the Son and the Son's union with the Father. See to what a glorious height our humanity has risen through Christ. By the grace of God, you who were like stones in the brook are made sons of God. Lifted out of your dead materialism, you are elevated into a spiritual life, and you are united to God. You have not any idea of what God has already done for you, and truly it does not yet appear what you shall be. A Christian man is the noblest work of God. God has here reached the fullness of His power and His grace in making us to be one with His own dear Son, and so bringing us into union and communion with Himself. Oh, if the words that I speak could convey to you the fullness of their own meaning, you might spring to your feet electrified with holy joy to think of this, that we should be Christ's, and the Father's, and that we should be thought worthy to be the object of intricate transactions and intercommunions of the dearest kind between the Father and the Son! We, even we, who are but dust and ashes at our very best, are favored as angels never were. Therefore let all praise be ascribed to Sovereign grace!

The Glory of Christ

And now I shall only detain you a few minutes longer while I speak upon the third part of our subject, that is, "And I am glorified in them." I must confess that while the former part of my subject was very deep, this third part seems to me to be deeper still, "I am glorified in them."

If Christ had said, "I will glorify them," I could have understood it. If He had said, "I am pleased with them," I might have set it down to His great kindness to them. But when He says, "I am glorified in them," it is very wonderful. The sun can be reflected, but you need proper objects to act as reflectors. The brighter they are, the better will they reflect. You and I do not seem to have the power of reflecting Christ's glory. We break up the glorious rays that shine upon us. We spoil, we ruin so much of the good that falls upon us. Yet Christ says that He is glorified in us. Take these words home, dear friend, to yourself. Think that the Lord Jesus met you tonight, and as you went out of the Tabernacle said to you, "Thou art mine, thou art my Father's; and I am glorified in thee." I dare not say that it would be a proud moment for you. But I dare to say that there would be more in it to make you feel exalted for Him to say, "I am glorified in you," than if you could have all the honors that all the kings can put upon all men in the world. I think that I could say, "Lord, now lettest thou thy servant depart in peace, according to thy word" (Luke 2:29), if He would but say to me, "I am glorified in your ministry." I hope that He is. I believe that He is. But, oh, for an assuring word, if not spoken to us personally, yet spoken to His Father about us as in our text, "I am glorified in them"!

How can this be? Well, it is a very wide subject. Christ is glorified in His people in many ways. *He is glorified by saving such sinners,* taking these people, so sinful, so lost, so unworthy. When the Lord lays hold upon a drunkard, a thief, an adulterer; when He arrests one who has been guilty of blasphemy, whose very heart is reeking with evil thoughts; when He picks up the far-off one, the abandoned, the dissolute, the fallen, as He often does; and when He says, "These shall be mine. I will wash these in my blood. I will use these to speak my word," oh, then He is glorified in them! Read the lives of many great sinners who have afterward become great saints, and you will see how they have tried to glorify Him, not only she who washed His feet with her tears, but many another like her. Oh, how they have loved to praise Him! Eyes have wept tears, lips have spoken words, but hearts have felt what neither eyes nor lips could speak of adoring gratitude to Him. "I am glorified in them." Great sinners, Christ is glorified in you. Some of you Pharisees, if you were to be converted, would not bring Christ such glory as He gets through saving publicans and harlots. Even if you struggled into heaven, it would be with very little music for Him on the road, certainly no tears and no ointment for His feet, and no wiping them with the hairs of your head. You are too respectable ever to do that. But when He saves great sinners, He can truly say, "I am glorified in them," and each of them can sing—

> It passeth praises, that dear love of thine,
> My Jesus, Savior: yet this heart of mine
> Would sing that love, so full, so rich, so free,
> Which brings a rebel sinner, such as me,
> Nigh unto God.

And *Christ is glorified by the perseverance which He shows in the matter of their salvation.* See how He begins to save and the man resists. He follows up His kind endeavor, and the man rebels. He hunts him, pursues him, dogs his footsteps. He will have the man, and the man will not have him. But the Lord, without violating the free will of man, which He never does, yet at length brings the one who was most unwilling to lie at His feet. He that hated most begins to love, and he that was most stouthearted bows the knee in lowliest humility. It is wonderful how persevering the Lord is in the salvation of a sinner. Aye, and in the salvation of His own, for you would have broken loose long ago if your great Shepherd had not penned you up within the fold. Many of you would have started aside and have lost yourselves if it had not been for constraints of sovereign grace which have kept you to this day and will not let you go. Christ is glorified in you. Oh, when you once get to heaven, when the angels know all that you were and all that you tried to be, when the whole story of almighty, infinite grace is told, as it will be told, then will Christ be glorified in you!

Beloved, *we actively glorify Christ when we display Christian graces.* You who are loving, forgiving, tenderhearted, gentle, meek, self-sacrificing, you glorify Him. He is glorified in you. You who are upright and who will not be moved from your integrity, you who can despise the sinner's gold and will not sell your conscience for it, you who are bold and brave for Christ, you who can bear and suffer for His name's sake, all your graces come from Him. As all the flowers are bred and begotten of the sun, so all that is in you that is good comes from Christ, the Sun of righteousness. Therefore He is glorified in you.

But, beloved, God's people have glorified Christ in many other ways. *When they make Him the object of all their trust, they glorify Him.* When they say, "Though I am the chief of sinners, yet I trust Him. Though my mind is dark, and though my temptations abound, I believe that He can save to the uttermost. I do trust Him." Christ is more glorified by a sinner's humble faith than by a seraph's loudest song. If you believe, you do glorify Him. Child of God, are you very dark, dull, and heavy? Do you feel half dead spiritually? Come to your Lord's feet and kiss them, and believe that He can save—no, that He has saved you, even you. Thus you will glorify His holy name. "Oh!" said a believer the other day, "'I know whom I have believed' (2 Tim. 1:12). Christ is mine." "Ah!" said another, "that is presumption." Beloved, it is nothing of the kind. It is not presumption for a child to own his own father. It might be pride for him to be ashamed of his father. It is certainly great alienation from his father if he is ashamed to own him. "I know whom I have believed." Happy state of heart, to be absolutely sure that you are resting upon Christ, that He is your Savior, that you believe in Him, for Jesus said, "He that believeth on me hath everlasting life" (John 6:47). I believe on Him, and I have everlasting life. "He that believeth on him is not condemned" (John 3:18). I believe on Him, and I am not condemned. Make sure work of this, not only by signs and evidences, but do even better. Make the one sign and the one evidence to be this, "Jesus Christ came into the world to save sinners. I, a sinner, accept His great sacrifice, and I am saved."

Especially, I think that *God's people glorify Christ by a cheerful conversation.* If you go about moaning and mourning, pining and complaining, you bring no honor to His name. But if, when you fast, you appear not to men to fast, if you can wear a cheerful countenance, even when your heart is heavy, and if, above all, you can rally your spirit out of its depths and begin to bless God when the cupboard is empty and friends are few, then you will indeed glorify Christ.

Many are the ways in which this good work may be done. Let us try to do it. "I am glorified in them," says Christ; that is, *by their bold confession of Christ.* Do I address myself to any here who love Christ, but who have never owned it? Do come out, and come out very soon. He deserves to have all the glory that you can give Him. If He has healed you, be not like the nine who forgot that Christ had healed their leprosy. Come and praise the name of the great Healer, and let others know what Christ can do. I am afraid that there are a great many here tonight who hope that they are Christians, but they have never said so. What are you ashamed of? Ashamed of your Lord? I am afraid that you do not, after all, love Him. Now, at this time, at this particular crisis of the history of the church and world, if we do not publicly take sides with

Christ, we shall really be against Him. The time is come now when we cannot afford to have go-betweens. You must be for Him or for His enemies. He asks you if you are really His, to say it. Come forward, unite yourself with His people, and let it be seen by your life and conversation that you do belong to Christ. If not, how can it be true, "I am glorified in them"? Is Christ glorified in a non-confessing people, a people that hope to go slinking into heaven by the by-roads or across the fields, but dare not come into the King's highway and travel with the King's subjects, and own that they belong to Him?

Lastly, I think that *Christ is glorified in His people by their efforts to extend His kingdom.* What efforts are you making? There is a great deal of force in a church like this. But I am afraid that there is a great deal of waste steam, waste power here. The tendency is, so often, to leave everything to be done by the minister, or else by one or two leading people. But I do pray you, beloved, if you be Christ's, and if you belong to the Father, if, unworthy though you be, you are claimed with a double ownership by the Father and the Son, do try to be of use to them. Let it be seen by your winning others to Christ that He is glorified in you. I believe that by diligent attendance to even the smallest Sunday school class, Christ is glorified in you. By that private conversation in your own room, by that letter which you dropped into the post with many a prayer, by anything that you have done with a pure motive, trusting in God in order to glorify Christ, He is glorified in you.

Do not mistake my meaning with regard to serving the Lord. I think it exceedingly wrong when I hear exhortations made to young people, "Quit your service as domestics, and come out into spiritual work. Businessmen, leave your shops. Workmen, give up your trades. You cannot serve Christ in that calling, come away from it altogether." I beg to say that nothing will be more pestilent than such advice as that. There are men called by the grace of God to separate themselves from every earthly occupation, and they have special gifts for the work of the ministry. But ever to imagine that the bulk of Christian people cannot serve God in their daily calling is to think altogether contrary to the mind of the Spirit of God. If you are a servant, remain a servant. If you are a waiter, go on with your waiting. If you are a tradesman, go on with your trade. Let every man abide in the calling wherein he is called, unless there be to him some special call from God to devote himself to the ministry. Go on with your employment, dear Christian people, and do not imagine that you are to turn hermits or monks or nuns. You would not glorify God if you did so act. Soldiers of Christ are to fight the battle out where they are. To quit the field and shut yourselves up alone would be to render it impossible that you should get the victory. The work of God is as holy and acceptable in domestic service, or in trade, as any service that can be rendered in the pulpit, or even by the foreign missionary.

We thank God for the men specially called and set apart for His own work. But we know that they would do nothing unless the salt of our holy faith should permeate the daily life of other Christians. You godly mothers, you are the glory of the church of Christ. You hard working men and women who endure patiently "as seeing him who is invisible" (Heb. 11:27), are the crown and glory of the church of God. You who do not shirk your daily labor, but stand manfully to it, obeying Christ in it, are proving what the Christian religion was meant to do.

We can, if we are truly priests to God, make our everyday garments into vestments, our meals into sacraments, and our houses into temples for God's worship. Our very beds will be within the veil, and our inmost thoughts will be as a sweet incense perpetually smoking up to the Most High. Dream not that there is anything about any honest calling that degrades a man or hinders him in glorifying God. But sanctify it all, until the bells upon the horses shall ring out, "Holiness to the Lord," and the pots in your houses shall be as holy as the vessels of the sanctuary.

Now, I want that we should so come to the communion-table that even here Christ may be glorified in us. Ah, you may sit at the Lord's table wearing a fine dress or a diamond ring, and you may think that you are somebody of importance, but you are not! Ah, you may come to the Lord's table and say, "Here is an experienced Christian man who knows a thing or two." You are not glorifying Christ that way. You are only a nobody. But if you come tonight saying, "Lord, I am hungry. You can feed me," that is glorifying Him. If you come saying, "Lord, I have no merit and no worthiness, I come because You have died for me, and I trust You," you are glorifying Him. He glorifies Christ most who takes most from Him, and who then gives most back to Him. Come, empty pitcher, come and be filled. When you are filled, pour all out at the dear feet of Him who filled you. Come, trembler, come and let Him touch you with His strengthening hand. Then go out and work, and use the strength which He has given you. I fear that I have not led you where I wanted to bring you, close to my Lord and to the Father, yet I have done my best. May the Lord forgive my feebleness and wandering, and yet bless you for His dear name's sake! Amen.

8

Christ's Negative and Positive Prayer

I pray not that thou shouldest take them out of the world, but that thou shouldest keep them from the evil (John 17:15).

Notice in the prayer of our Divine Lord what honor He always puts upon God the Father. He ascribes to God everything—the taking the disciples out of the world or the keeping them from the evil in the world. Let us never neglect to look for God's hand in all that happens to the saints. Let us not fall into the error of those who deny the Great First Cause and are always dealing with appearances, forgetting the Mighty God who shapes our ends and rules our destinies. If we die, it is not by chance, but because God takes us out of the world. Believers fall asleep in Jesus, neither before nor after the predestined time. No disease or accident can cut short their lives. It would not be possible to prolong their existence beyond the time appointed by the Lord. I like to believe—whatever it may be to some of you, to me it is very sweet to believe that—

All must come, and last, and end,
As shall please my heavenly Friend.

Plagues and deaths around me fly,
Until he bids I cannot die:
Not a single shaft can hit
Until the God of love thinks fit.

Our lives are entirely in the keeping of our loving Father. You can see that truth in the text. Jesus speaks of God as taking the beloved ones out of the world, and it is even so. This fact should make us cease to be

This sermon was taken from *The Metropolitan Tabernacle Pulpit* and was preached on Sunday evening, January 22, 1882.

88

anxious about when or how we shall die. It should, at the same time, reconcile us to the time and the manner of the home-going of any whom we love most dearly. They were not snatched away by the robber Death. They were taken out of the world by our dear Father's gracious hand. Let us say concerning them what Job said of His loved ones, "The LORD gave, and the LORD hath taken away; blessed be the name of the LORD" (1:21).

See, also, how our Lord Jesus honors the Father by ascribing to Him the keeping of the saints from evil, for He says, "I pray not that thou shouldest take them out of the world, but that thou shouldest keep them from the evil." Beloved, our escape from evil, at the first, was by the Father's grace. Our persevering in righteousness until now has been wrought in us by the Father's hand through the Divine Spirit. This day, if we have not apostatized, if we have not denied the faith and proved traitors to Christ, we must ascribe it entirely to the grace of God. As the psalmist says, "It is he that hath made us, and not we ourselves" (100:3). It is He who keeps us, and not we ourselves, for, again quoting the hundredth Psalm, "We are his people, and the sheep of his pasture" (v. 3).

I want you, as far as you possibly can, to be constantly recognizing God's overruling hand. God, in our death, taking us out of the world, and God, in our life, keeping us from evil and upholding us in our integrity. When you get thus near to God and realize that God is ever present with you, you are in the right frame of mind for prayer. You are also in the state and condition of heart which will give you courage in time of danger. You are, indeed, ready for anything and for everything, whatever may come to you, when God is thus consciously overshadowing your spirit. This much, I think, the prayer of our Lord plainly suggests.

Observe, again, that God has us absolutely at His disposal. Let us ever remember that great truth. The prayer of Jesus recognizes His Father's sovereignty, but we ourselves must also recognize that we are entirely in God's hand. He can take us out of the world, or He can keep us in the world and preserve us from the evil. We are glad to be at the disposal of our God. As His people, we would have no voice or choice in fixing our own position, but with the psalmist we would say, "He shall choose our inheritance for us" (Ps. 47:4). Whether we stay or whether we go depends entirely upon the Lord's will. Christ in His prayer recognizes that it is so. He would not pray for a matter which was not in the hand of Him to whom He prayed. So felt that His people were absolutely at His Father's disposal, and therefore, He presented the prayer that is to be the subject of our meditation tonight.

Now, in this petition, there are two things. There is, first, *the negative prayer:* "I pray not that thou shouldest take them out of the world." Then, secondly, there is *the positive prayer:* "But that thou shouldest keep them from the evil."

The Negative Prayer

"I pray not that thou shouldest take them out of the world." At first sight that seems almost unkind on our Savior's part. What could happen better than for those whom the world hated to be taken out of the world? Jesus Himself was going out of the world. What could He do that should have greater love in it than to pray that they might go with Him? I have often felt as Thomas did when he said, "Let us also go, that we may die with him" (John 11:16). Has Jesus gone? Why should we tarry here? Has Jesus entered the glory? Let us be with Him where He is that we may behold His glory. There is nothing left to detain us below since He has ascended to His Father's right hand. But there is everything to attract us upward since He is there who is our heart's Lord, our all in all. Have you not often felt inclined to pray for yourself that the Lord would take you out of the world? I mean, not merely in times of depression, when, like Elijah, who never died, you are ready to pray, "Now, O LORD, take away my life" (1 Kings 19:4). But in times of exultation when you have been near to the gates of heaven in ecstatic joy and holy gladness, have you not wished to slip in? "Lord, it is good for us to be here: if thou wilt, let us make here three tabernacles" (Matt. 17:4). Have you not said so in your heart, if not with your voice? No, have you not wished not to stay on the Mount of Transfiguration, but from that point to take your heavenward flight and land yourself in the New Jerusalem, to go no more out forever? I know that, sometimes, on a Sunday when we have been singing to the tune *Prospect*—

> On Jordan's stormy banks I stand,
> And cast a wishful eye
> To Canaan's fair and happy land,
> Where my possessions lie—

I have felt that I could from my heart sing the last verse of the hymn—

> Fill'd with delight, my raptured soul
> Can here no longer stay:
> Though Jordan's waves around me roll,
> Fearless I'd launch away.

Yet the Savior says, "I pray not that thou shouldest take them out of the world." I am sure, therefore, that it is a better thing for us to stop here until our appointed time than it is for us to be taken out of the world. It may not be better in all respects, but there are some points in which it is an advantage for believers to remain here. Our Savior loves us so much that He would be certain to ask the very best thing for us. Therefore, for us to be taken out of the world at once would not be, all things considered, the best disposition of us that the Lord could make.

How is that? Well, first, if we, who are Christ's people, were taken out of the world, then *the world itself would perish.* Do we contemplate, with any pleasure, such a catastrophe as that? "Ye are the light of the world" (Matt. 5:14). Take all the lights away and the murky atmosphere, which is dark enough even now, would become dense as Egyptian midnight, and life would be intolerable. "Ye are the salt of the earth" (v. 13). Should the salt be taken away, putrefaction would revel without limit, and corruption would then have nothing to contend with it. The world would reek in the nostrils of God Himself until He would be obliged to destroy it.

I look along the ages, and I see mankind given up to debauchery and eaten up with worldliness. Yet the sinners are permitted to live on year after year. But I also see a strange-looking ship that has been built on dry land. I watch the only family in the earth that fears God going up into that queerly-shaped vessel, and the door is shut by God Himself. I hear it as it closes. And the moment that door is shut, what happens? The world is doomed. God pulls up the sluices of the great deep that lies under, and He throws open the floodgates of heaven. The fountains gush up from below, and the rains pour down from above, until the whole world is drowned. This awful judgment did not begin until Noah, the one righteous man, was taken away from the rest of mankind and shut in the ark: "*The same day* were all the fountains of the great deep broken up, and the windows of heaven were opened. And the rain was upon the earth forty days and forty nights. *In the selfsame day* entered Noah, and Shem, and Ham, and Japheth, the sons of Noah, and Noah's wife, and the three wives of his sons with them, into the ark" (Gen. 7:11–13).

I look again and away yonder, I behold, in the vale of Siddim, the cities of Sodom and Gomorrah. If I go within their gates, I hear and see that which disgusts my soul. Things that it were a shame even to speak of are done in those cities. There is one good man who lives there, and only one. I see him, early one morning, flying with his wife and daughters out of the city. The moment he has passed beyond the bounds of the condemned cities and escaped to little Zoar, what happens? Destruction is poured out of heaven upon the guilty people: "The sun was risen upon the earth when Lot entered into Zoar. *Then* the LORD rained upon Sodom and upon Gomorrah brimstone and fire from the LORD out of heaven; and he overthrew those cities, and all the plain, and all the inhabitants of the cities, and that which grew upon the ground" (Gen. 19:23–25).

Because we do not wish such awful destruction as that, either by water or by fire, to fall upon this guilty world, we ask God to permit the salt to remain in the earth, the light still to burn in it, the Noah still to linger, the Lot still to dwell here yet a little while. When the Lord shall begin rapidly to gather His saints home, as He may do by-and-by, and when the wail is heard, "The faithful fail from among the children of men" (Ps. 12:1), then shall come dark days indeed. The earth shall know the terrible vengeance of Almighty God.

This, then, is one reason why Christ does not pray that we should be taken out of the world, because it would be the ruin of guilty men if the saints were removed from the earth which is only preserved for their sake.

Does not the Lord also wish the righteous to stay in the world a while that *they may be the means of the salvation of others?* How came Jesus here Himself? He came to seek and to save that which was lost. When He went away He did not take His disciples out of the world because their ministry was to be blessed to many of their fellow-creatures. In this very prayer to His Father He said, "As thou hast sent me into the world, even so have I also sent them into the world" (John 17:18). They who might be safely housed in heaven stay here that they may be the means of saving others. Mother is still here, though her son has well near broken her heart. She is left on the earth that she may yet win that boy for Christ. And our old gray-headed friend, whose infirmities are multiplying, is still among us, though he would be far happier among the harps of angels. But he is detained here that his grandson, or his still unconverted daughter, may hear from his lips once more a loving, living testimony for the Lord Jesus and may thereby be turned to God.

I do think that there are many of you, who do not yourselves love the Lord, who, nevertheless, ought to be very grateful to Him for saying, "I pray not that thou shouldest take them out of the world." Oh, dear man, you do not want to lose that loving wife of yours! She has brought you here tonight after a good deal of coaxing and tender persuasion. You do not think of her God or care about the Lord Jesus, but your wife is still living to seek the salvation of your soul. I believe she will win you yet, by God's grace. There are many who might, long ago, have received their reward and would have been thrice happy to do so. But they have yet to preach the everlasting Gospel, and yet to win more souls to Christ. It is more needful for sinners that Paul should abide in the flesh a little longer, though he himself has a desire to depart and to be with Christ, which is far better.

Beloved Christian brothers and sisters, if the Lord is keeping any of us here with the object of using us in the salvation of others, let us take care that we answer the purpose of our continued existence on the earth. Let us be up and doing, let us be earnestly seeking the souls of our relatives, let us be zealously endeavoring to bring others to Christ. I am sometimes saddened when I hear of households conducted by professedly Christian people (places where one would think that God's name would be upon every tongue), and yet servants may live for years in such families, and their masters and mistresses never speak to them about their souls. And many men, employing hundreds of work people, will give them their wages as if they had no souls to care about. For they take no interest in the eternal welfare of those who work for them in temporal things. Do not let it be so with you, dear friends. Masters and mistresses, there are occasions in which you can go to your servants, and those employed by you, and without being at all intrusive, can seek to interest them in the things of God. You can call at their homes, perhaps. The offering of a prayer and speaking to them about the Gospel of Christ may reach them and bring them to the Savior, where our sermons have failed to do so. I charge you, by Him who bought you by His blood, either go to heaven and glorify Christ there, or else, if you remain in the world, glorify Him here. But whether you live or whether you die, do see to this matter, that you answer the divine purpose which is that, being saved yourself, you may become the means of saving others.

There is a second reason, then, for our Lord wishing His disciples to stop here, that they may be the means of the salvation of others.

Next, I think the Lord lets His people stay in the world that *they may serve Him in the place where they sinned against Him*. If I had been converted just now, and the Lord were to open the gates of heaven and say, "Come in," I think that I should step back and say, "Dear Master, may I stop here just a little while to undo some of the mischief that I did in my ungodly state?" I can fancy that someone here would pray, "Lord, there is my friend who used to go to the theater and the music hall with me, and I taught him much that was mischievous. Will it please You to let me tarry here and tell him about Your great salvation?" I think that another would say, "Lord, I spent so many years in the service of the Devil. Now, before I go home to see Your face, let me have a few years in Your service! I would like to undo at least a portion of the evil that I have done before I stand in your presence amid the eternal splendors of heaven." It seems to me that it is most gracious of the Lord to let us remain here to serve Him where we sinned against Him, and not to take us home as soon as we are converted. I think that we shall congratulate ourselves even in heaven that we had some opportunity of contending for the faith, or of bearing reproach for Christ's sake, or of seeking to win souls for Him before we entered upon our everlasting rest.

Is not that a good reason why the Savior did not pray that His disciples might be taken out of the world?

And is not this another good reason why saints are left in the world? *The Lord keeps His people here that He may exhibit in them the power of divine grace.* Just as He permitted Job to be tempted of the Devil that all the world might see how God can enable a man by patience to triumph, so He keeps us here to let the Devil and all men know what His grace can do for His people, and also to let angels and principalities and powers in the heavenly places behold what saints God can make out of guilty sinners. He takes those who had gone far away in sin and brings them near by the blood of Jesus. He fashions the rough, knotty timber that did not seem as if it ever could be shaped and uses it in the building of His temple. He makes wonders of grace out of sinful men and women, such marvels of mercy that the angels will stand and gaze at them throughout eternity as they say, "How could God make such perfect beings as these out of such sinful material?" All this will be "to the praise of the glory of his grace, wherein he hath made us accepted in the beloved" (Eph. 1:6). You see, we cannot exhibit patience in heaven. So far as we now know anything about heaven, it does not seem possible that there will be any need of patience there. We cannot manifest strength of faith in heaven, for faith will be lost in sight. We *can* take our love into glory. There are some flowers that will sweetly open in the land where they have no need of the sun, for Christ is better than the sun. There are certain flowers of less sweet perfume, and those can only be developed in the earth. The Lord, therefore, bids us tarry here awhile that He may show what grace can do in sustaining us in suffering, upholding us under trial, and protecting us against temptation. O soldiers of the Cross, do you want crowns without having contended for them?

> Must you be carried to the skies
> On flowery beds of ease;
> While others fought to win the prize,
> And sailed through bloody seas?

Ask no such thing. Be satisfied to take your share in the conflict, or else I do not see how you can so sweetly relish the triumph which God will give to His people in due time.

Thus, the Lord exhibits the power of His grace in us. That is another reason why we have to tarry here a while.

Next, I shall have to say many things very briefly where I could have wished to have had time for enlargement. Do you not think that we are kept here *to prepare us for heaven?* Are we not as yet like children who need education for that truer, higher life? When a boy first goes to school, you do not put into his hand the higher classics. He must plod through his grammar and must learn many elementary lessons. Then he must work hard on dry and dreary roots, and afterward you will give him some classic poet that he may read intelligently. So must you and I, here below, go plodding through our primers. We must work hard at our grammars and must have a slate and pencil still. When we have become proficient in all we have to learn here, we shall the better enjoy the holy rest and perfect service that make up the heaven of the blessed.

Let me give you an illustration of what I mean. A boy is sent to school, and his parents pinch themselves to pay for him to have a good education. It is not every boy who will say this to himself, but if he does, he is a first-rate lad: "My poor father and mother are doing all they can to give me a first-class education here. They want to make something of me. I am going to learn with all my heart, so that I may be worthy of all that my parents design for me, and not waste one single shilling of the money they are spending upon me." Such a boy is diligent at his books. He labors where others loiter, and treasures up in his mind everything that he learns while others forget it. Now the Lord Jesus Christ is thus putting some of us to school, training us for high employment hereafter. He means to make something of us by-and-by. Our desire now is to be prepared as far as possible for what Christ intends for us that we may be the more to His praise and glory, and our own completeness forever and ever.

I have often been puzzled by those words of the Lord Jesus, "I go to prepare a place for you" (John 14:2). What there was about heaven that was not ready, I do not know, except it was that Jesus Himself was not there. But I can easily understand this truth, that we are not ready for heaven yet, for heaven consists more in character than in place. We have to be more completely sanctified, more truly developed in all good things than we are at present. We are not yet fit for the glory land, so Jesus does not pray that we should be taken out of the world. But we are to wait here a little longer until His grace has more fully fitted us for glory.

Does not the Lord also, by keeping us here, mean us *to see more of the wisdom, the power, the grace, and the truth of God?* Within this last month—a month of remarkable pain and travail to me—I have had certain experiences which I shall never forget. I would pass through seas ten times as deep and boisterous merely for the sake of having those experiences repeated. There are some of them that I could not tell here. There are facts connected with them that would be discreditable to some who had to do with them, though greatly honorable to others. But as to my God, they have shown me His faithfulness, His power, His tenderness, His wisdom. I believe that had I been in heaven I should not have seen as much of some of the attributes of God as I have seen here below. If you had been an angel, forever praising God in glory, could you tell how faithful He is to a tried saint? Could you say, if you had not experienced it here on earth, how surely He comforts His people in their deepest sorrows? There are some pearls in these troubled waters that the sea of glass itself can never contain. There are some bright eternal lessons that we should never have known, if it had not been for our earthly trials, even if we might have had an archangel for a schoolmaster. Therefore, we must stop here a while and suffer affliction, temptation, depression of spirit, and slander and abuse that we may learn thereby the deeper truths of God's revelation.

I shall have to abandon the second part of my subject, I see, for my time has nearly gone already. I must, however, make just one more remark upon our first head.

I think that our Lord Jesus does not pray that we may be called out of the world because *He knows that we shall be taken to heaven in due time.* He scarcely thinks of that as a matter of prayer. It is so entirely in the Father's hands that He leaves it there. I would not encourage anybody here to pray that He might die. On the other hand, I do not know that I would incite anybody here to pray very earnestly that He might live. Hezekiah prayed that his life might be lengthened, and his prayer was granted. Manasseh would not have been born if Hezekiah had not lived those extra fifteen years. It would have been a good thing if Manasseh had never been born. Those sins and iniquities with which he made Judah to sin with his idols, though they were forgiven, yet filled up the cup of the nation's perversion from God and fixed the doom of that apostate people. I do not know, if the lifting of our finger could make us live for another twenty years, whether we had not better hesitate to lift that finger.

At any rate, I feel quite clear about the other side of the question, we have no business to pray that we may die. As I have already reminded you, the man who did pray that he might die never died at all. How foolish he was to pray that he might die when God had intended that he should go to heaven by a whirlwind with a chariot and horses of fire! We shall die all in good time, unless the Lord shall come in the splendor of His Second Advent. If you and I had the choice of the time of our death, there would be just a tinge of the element of suicide about it, and that is the very worst form of murder. This is clearly our duty, to leave ourselves wholly and unreservedly in the hand of Him to whom belong the issues of life. It is certainly our best course.

This, then, is our Lord's negative prayer: "I pray not that thou shouldest take them out of the world."

The Positive Prayer

What did Jesus pray for His disciples? That God would keep them from the evil. This is the right prayer for you to offer for yourself. Do not pray to get out of the battle. Ask of God that you may never be a coward, but that you may bravely play the man in the day of danger. Do not seek to be screened from affliction, but plead that you may never be driven to sin by your affliction. You need not even pray that you may not have prosperity, but you may entreat the Lord that prosperity may not make you proud or worldly. Let your condition be as God wills it. But let your great anxiety be that you may be kept from all sin in every condition.

"I pray not that thou shouldest take them out of the world, but that thou shouldest keep them from the evil." We need to be kept from the evil of *apostasy,* the evil of *worldliness,* from the evil of *unholiness,* from the evil of getting to be as men of the world are. That is the main point. I do not think that it matters much what the condition of a man is as long as his heart is above his condition. I remember that St. Bernard, as he is usually called—Bernard, of Clairvaux—one of the holiest and humblest of men, was one day riding on a mule to a certain monastery. One who saw him said, "I think Bernard is getting proud, because he is riding on a mule, and sitting upon a cloth which has a fringe of gold lace to it." Now Bernard was a man who cared nothing for that sort of thing. When the other charged him with pride he said, "Perhaps it may be so, but I never noticed that I had any cloth at all." Someone else had put that fine cloth upon the mule without his knowing anything about it. He really thought that he was riding on the animal's bare back, for his mind was taken up with something far more important.

If you are rich and have a cloth with a gold fringe to it, do not be conscious of its existence. Let your soul rise above it. If you are poor and have no saddle at all, do not notice your lack. Let your soul soar above such matters. Pray not that you may be taken out of this or that, be it poverty or be it wealth, be it sickness or be it health. But pray that you may be kept from the evil of it, for there is an evil in every case. If you are making money, we ought to have a special prayer meeting for you to pray that you may be kept from evil. I said to a brother who was going to a banquet the other day, "Well, we will pray for you, dear friend, for you are going into a place of peril." I do not think there was any great risk to such a man in going. Perhaps some of those who stopped at home and complained of him were in more danger. The great point is, not where you are, not what you are as to circumstances, but that you may be kept by almighty power from the evil which might come out of any circumstances unless you were divinely preserved from the evil. Oh, that the Lord Jesus may say this concerning us tonight: "I pray not that thou shouldest take them out of the world, but that thou shouldest keep them from the evil"! If so, we can leave everything else in His dear hands.

But, friends, do not let us be anxious to get to heaven just yet. Let us seek to fight our way there in valiant fashion. Do not let us be so earnest about the end as about the way, laying hold on Christ and uplifting His dear cross as our banner. Oh, that all of you would do this and follow the Lamb whithersoever He goes! We will just bend our thoughts to this one point and not think so much of going to heaven as of avoiding sin. Lord, keep me out of evil! Then let me live or let me die, hold me up or press me down, let me dance with joy of heart, or let me lie and pine in an agony of pain, with anguish racking every bone in my body, it shall be all the same to me. So long as nothing of the evil of surrounding circumstances enters into me, do with me as You will, O my God!

God bless you, dear friends, for Jesus' sake! Amen.

9

The Character of Christ's People

They are not of the world, even as I am not of the world (John 17:16).

Christ's prayer was for a special people. He declared that He did not offer a universal intercession. "I pray for *them*," said He. "I pray not for the world, but for them which thou hast given me; for they are thine" (John 17:9). In reading this beautiful prayer through only one question arises to our minds, Who are the people that are described as "them" or as "they?" Who are these favored individuals, who share a Savior's prayers, are recognized by a Savior's love, have their names written on the stones of His precious breastplate, and have their characters and their circumstances mentioned by the lips of the High Priest before the throne on high? The answer to that question is supplied by the words of our text. The people for whom Christ prays are an unearthly people. They are a people somewhat above the world, distinguished altogether from it. "They are not of the world, even as I am not of the world" (v. 14).

I shall treat my text, first of all, *doctrinally;* secondly, *experimentally;* and thirdly, *practically.*

Doctrinally

The doctrine of it is that God's people are a people who are not of the world, even as Christ was not of the world. It is not so much that they are not of the world as that they are "not of the world, *even as Christ was not of the world.*" This is an important distinction, for there are to be found certain people who are not of the world, and yet they

---

This sermon was taken from *The New Park Street Pulpit* and was preached on Thursday evening, November 22, 1855.

99

are not Christians. Among those I would mention sentimentalists—people who are always crying and groaning in affected sentimental ways. Their spirits are so refined, their characters are so delicate, that they could not attend to ordinary business. They would think it rather degrading to their spiritual nature to attend to anything connected with the world. They live much in the air of romances and novels. They love to read things that fetch tears from their eyes. They would like continually to live in a cottage near a wood or to inhabit some quiet cave where they could read "Zimmerman on Solitude" forever, for they feel that they are "not of the world." The fact is, there is something too flimsy about them to stand the wear and tear of this wicked world. They are so preeminently good that they cannot bear to do as we poor human creatures do. I have heard of one young lady, who thought herself so spiritually-minded that she could not work. A very wise minister said to her, "That is quite correct! You are so spiritually-minded that you cannot work. Very well, you are so spiritually-minded that you shall not eat unless you do." That brought her back from her great spiritual-mindedness.

There is a stupid sentimentalism that certain persons nurse themselves into. They read a parcel of books that intoxicate their brains, and then fancy that they have a lofty destiny. These people are "not of the world," truly. But the world does not want them, and the world would not miss them much if they were clean gone forever. There is such a thing as being "not of the world" from high order of sentimentalism, and yet not being a Christian after all. For it is not so much being "not of the world," as being "not of the world, *even as Christ* was not of the world." There are others, too, like your monks and those other mad individuals of the Catholic church who are not of the world. They are so awfully good that they could not live with us sinful creatures at all. They must be distinguished from us altogether. They must not wear, of course, a boot that would at all approach to a worldly shoe, but they must have a sole of leather strapped on with two or three thongs like the far-famed Father Ignatius. They could not be expected to wear worldly coats and waistcoats. But they must have peculiar garbs, cut in certain fashions, like the Passionists. They must wear particular dresses, particular garments, particular habits. And we know that some men are "not of the world," by the peculiar mouthing they give to all their words—the sort of sweet, savory, buttery flavor they give to the English language because they think themselves so eminently sanctified that they fancy it would be wrong to indulge in anything in which ordinary mortals indulge. Such persons are, however, reminded that their being "not of the world" has nothing to do with it. It is not being "not of the world" so much as being "not of the world, even as Christ was not of the world."

This is the distinguishing mark—being different from the world in those respects in which Christ was different. Not making ourselves singular in unimportant points as those poor creatures do, but being different from the world in those respects in which the Son of God and the Son of man, Jesus Christ, our glorious Exemplar, was distinguished from the rest of mankind. And I think this will burst out in great clearness and beauty to us if we consider that Christ was not of the world in nature; that He was not of the world again, in office; and above all, that He was not of the world in His character.

First, *Christ was not of the world in nature.* What was there about Christ that was worldly? In one point of view His nature was divine. As divine, it was perfect, pure, unsullied, spotless. He could not descend to things of earthliness and sin. In another sense He was human. His human nature, which was born of the Virgin Mary, was begotten of the Holy Spirit, and therefore was so pure that in it rested nothing that was worldly. He was not like ordinary men. We are all born with worldliness in our hearts. Solomon well says, "Foolishness is bound in the heart of a child" (Prov. 22:15). It is not only there, but it is bound up in it. It is tied up in his heart and is difficult to remove. And so with each of us, when we were children, earthliness and carnality were bound up in our nature. But Christ was not so. His nature was not a worldly one. It was essentially different from that of everyone else, although He sat down and talked with them. Mark the difference! He stood side by side with a Pharisee, but everyone could see He was not of the Pharisee's world. He sat by a Samaritan woman. Though He conversed with her very freely, who is it that fails to see that He is not of that Samaritan woman's world—not a sinner like her? He mingled with the Publicans. No, He sat down at the Publican's feast, and ate with Publicans and sinners. But you could see by the holy actions and the peculiar gestures He there carried with Him that He was not of the Publicans' world, though He mixed with them. There was something so different in His nature that you could not have found an individual in all the world whom you could have set beside Him and said, "There He is of that man's world." No, not even John, though he leaned on His bosom and partook very much of his Lord's spirit was exactly of that world to which Jesus belonged. For even he once in his Boanergean spirit said words to this effect, "Let us call down fire from heaven on the heads of those who oppose You" (see Luke 9:54)—a thing that Christ could not endure for a moment, and thereby proved that He was something even beyond John's world.

Well, beloved, in some sense, the Christian man is not of the world even in his nature. I do not mean in his corrupt and fallen nature, but in his new nature. There is something in a Christian that is utterly and entirely distinct from that of anybody else. Many persons think that the difference between a Christian and a worldling consists in this: One goes to chapel twice on a Sunday, another does not go but once or perhaps not at all. One of them takes the sacrament, the other does not. One pays attention to holy things, the other pays very little attention to them. But, ah, beloved, that does not make a Christian. The distinction between a Christian and a worldling is not merely external, but internal. The difference is one of nature, and not of act.

A Christian is as essentially different from a worldling as a dove is from a raven, or a lamb from a lion. He is not of the world even in his nature. You could not make him a worldling. You might do what you liked. You might cause him to fall into some temporary sin, but you could not make him a worldling. You might cause him to backslide, but you could not make him a sinner as he used to be. He is not of the world by his nature. He is a twice-born man. In his veins run the blood of the royal family of the universe. He is a nobleman. He is a heaven-born child. His freedom is not merely a bought one, but he has his liberty by his new-born nature. He is begotten again to a lively hope. He is not of the world by his nature. He is essentially and entirely different from the world. There are persons in this chapel now who are more totally distinct from one another than you can even conceive. I have some here who are intelligent and some who are ignorant, some who are rich and some who are poor, but I do not allude to those distinctions. They all melt away into nothing in that great distinction—dead or alive, spiritual or carnal, Christian or worldling. And oh if you are God's people, then you are not of the world in your nature, for you are "not of the world, even as Christ was not of the world."

Again: *you are not of the world in your office.* Christ's office had nothing to do with worldly things. "Are You a king then?" Yes; I am a king, but My kingdom is not of this world. "Are You a priest?" Yes; I am a priest. But My priesthood is not the priesthood which I shall soon lay aside or which shall be discontinued as that of others has been. "Are You a teacher?" Yes; but My doctrines are not the doctrines of morality, doctrines that concern earthly dealings between man and man simply. My doctrine comes down from heaven. So Jesus Christ, we say, is "not of the world." He had no office that could be termed a worldly one, and He had no aim that was in the least worldly. He did not seek His own applause, His own fame, His own honor. His very office was not of the world.

And, O believer! what is your office? Have you none at all? Why, yes, man! You are a priest to the Lord your God. Your office is to offer a sacrifice of prayer and praise each day. Ask a Christian what he is. Say to him: "What is your official standing? What are you by office?" Well, if he answers you properly, he will not say, "I am a draper or druggist," or anything of that sort. No; he will say, "I am a priest to my God. The office to which I am called is to be the salt of the earth. I am a city set on a hill, a light that cannot be hid. That is my office. My office is not a worldly one." Whether yours be the office of the minister or the deacon or the church member, you are not of this world in your office, even as Christ was not of the world. Your occupation is not a worldly one.

Again, *you are not of the world in your character,* for that is the chief point in which Christ was not of the world. And now, friends, I shall have to turn somewhat from doctrine to practice before I get rightly to this part of the subject. For I must reprove many of the Lord's people that they do not sufficiently manifest that they are not of the world in character, even as Christ was not of the world. Oh! how many of you there are who will assemble around the table at the supper of your Lord who do not live like your Savior. How many of you there are who join our church and walk with us, and yet are not worthy of your high calling and profession. Mark you the churches all around, and let your eyes run with tears when you remember that of many of their members it cannot be said, "ye *are not* of the world," for they *are* of the world. O, my hearers, I fear many of you are worldly, carnal, and covetous. Yet you join the churches and stand well with God's people by a hypocritical profession. O you whitewashed sepulchers! you would deceive even the very elect! You make clean the outside of the cup and platter, but your inward part is very wickedness. O that a thundering voice might speak this to your ears!—"Those whom Christ loves are not of the world," but you are of the world. Therefore you cannot be His even though you profess so to be, for those that love Him are not such as you.

Look at Jesus' character, how different from every other man's— pure, perfect, spotless, even such should be the life of the believer. I plead not for the possibility of sinless conduct in Christians, but I must hold that grace makes men to differ, and that God's people will be very different from other kinds of people. A servant of God will be God's everywhere. As a chemist, he could not indulge in any tricks that such men might play with their drugs. As a grocer—if indeed it be not a phantom that such things are done—he could not mix sloe leaves with tea or red lead in the pepper. If he practiced any other kind of business, he could not for a moment condescend to the little petty shifts called "methods of business." To him it is nothing what is called "business." It is what is called God's law. He feels that he is not of the world, consequently, he goes against its fashions and its maxims. A singular story is told of a certain Quaker. One day he was bathing in the Thames, and a waterman called out to him, "Ha! there goes the Quaker." "How do you know I'm a Quaker?" "Because you swim against the stream. It is the way the Quakers always do." That is the way Christians always ought to do—to swim against the stream. The Lord's people should not go along with the rest in their worldliness. Their characters should be visibly different. You should be such men that your fellows can recognize you without any difficulty and say, "Such a man is a Christian."

Ah! beloved, it would puzzle the angel Gabriel himself to tell whether some of you are Christians or not if he were sent down to the world to pick out the righteous from the wicked. None but God could do it, for in these days of worldly religion they are so much alike. It was an ill day for the world when the sons of God and the daughters of men were mingled together. It is an ill day now when Christians and worldlings are so mixed that you cannot tell the difference between them. God save us from a day of fire that may devour us in consequence! But O beloved! the Christian will be always different from the world. This is a great doctrine, and it will be found as true in ages to come as in the centuries that are past. Looking back into history we read this lesson: "They are not of the world, even as I am not of the world." We see them driven to the catacombs of Rome. We see them hunted about like partridges. Wherever in history you find God's servants, you can recognize them by their distinct, unvarying character. They were not of the world, but were a people scarred and peeled, a people entirely distinct from the nations. And if in this age, there are no different people, if there are none to be found who differ from other people, there are no Christians. For Christians will be always different from the world. They are not of the world, even as Christ is not of the world. This is the doctrine.

Experimentally

Do we, dearly beloved, feel this truth? Has it ever been laid to our souls so that we can feel it is ours? "They are not of the world, even as I am not of the world." Have we ever felt that we are not of the world? Perhaps there is a believer sitting in a pew tonight who says, "Well, sir, I can't say that I feel as if I was not of the world. I have just come from my shop, and worldliness is still hanging about me." Another says, "I have been in trouble and my mind is very much harassed—I can't feel that I am different from the world. I am afraid that I am of the world." But, beloved, we must not judge ourselves rashly. because just at this moment we discern not the spot of God's children. Let me tell you, there are always certain testing moments when you can tell of what kind of stuff a man is made. Two men are walking. Part of the way their road lies side by side. How do you tell which man is going to the right and which to the left? Why, when they come to the turning point. Now, tonight is not a turning point, for you are sitting with worldly people here, but at other times we may distinguish.

Let me tell you one or two turning points when every Christian will feel that he is not of the world. One is, when he gets into very deep *trouble*. I do believe and protest that we never feel so unearthly as when we get plunged down into trouble. Ah! when some creature comfort has been swept away, when some precious blessing has withered in our sight like the fair lily snapped at the stalk, when some mercy has been withered like Jonah's gourd in the night—then it is that the Christian feels, "I am not of the world." His cloak is torn from him, and the cold wind whistles almost through him. Then he says, "I am a stranger in the world as all my fathers were. Lord, You have been my dwelling place in all generations." You have had at times deep sorrows. Thank God for them! They are testing moments. When the furnace is hot, it is then that the gold is tried best. Have you felt at such a time that you were not of the world? Or, have you rather sat down and said, "Oh! I do not deserve this trouble?" Did you break under it? Did you bow down before it and let it crush you while you cursed your Maker? Or did your spirit, even under its load, still lift itself to Him like a man all dislocated on the battlefield, whose limbs are cut away but still lifts himself up as best he can and looks over the field to see if there be a friend approaching. Did you do so? Or did you lie down in desperation and despair? If you did that, I think you are no Christian. But if there was a rising up, it was a testing moment, and it proved that you were "not of the world" because you could master affliction. You could tread it under foot and say—

> When all created streams are dry,
> His goodness is the same;
> With this I well am satisfied
> And glory in his name.

But another testing moment is *prosperity*. Oh! there have been some of God's people who have been more tried by prosperity than by adversity. Of the two trials, the trial of adversity is less severe to the spiritual man than that of prosperity. "As the fining pot for silver, so is a man to his praise." It is a terrible thing to be prosperous. You had need to pray to God, not only to help you in your troubles, but to help you in your blessings. Mr. Whitfield once had a petition to put up for a young man who had—stop, you will think it was for a young man who had lost his father or his property. No! "The prayers of the congregation are desired for a young man who has become heir to an immense fortune, and who feels he has need of much grace to keep him humble in the midst of riches." That is the kind of prayer that ought to be put up, for prosperity is a hard thing to bear. Now, perhaps you have become almost intoxicated with worldly delights, even as a Christian. Everything goes well with you. You have loved, and you are loved. Your affairs are prosperous. Your heart rejoices and your eyes sparkle. You tread the earth with a happy soul and a joyous countenance. You are a happy man, for you have found that even in worldly things "godliness with contentment is great gain" (1 Tim. 6:6). Did you ever feel—

> These can never satisfy;
> Give me Christ, or else I die.

Did you feel that these comforts were nothing but the leaves of the tree and not the fruit, and that you could not live upon mere leaves? Did you feel they were after all nothing but husks? Or did you not sit down and say, "Now, soul, take your ease. 'Thou hast much goods laid up for many years; eat, drink, and be merry' (Luke 12:19)?" If you did imitate the rich fool, then you were of the world. But if your spirit went up above your prosperity so that you still lived near to God, then you proved that you were a child of God, for you were not of the world. These are testing points—both prosperity and adversity.

Again: you may test yourselves in this way *in solitude and in company*. In solitude you may tell whether you are not of the world. I sit me down, throw the window up, look out on the stars, and think of them as the eyes of God looking down upon me! And oh! does it not seem glorious at times to consider the heaven. When we can say, "Ah! beyond those stars is my house not made with hands. Those stars are milestones on the road to glory. I shall soon tread the glittering way, or be carried by seraphs far beyond them and be there!" Have you felt in solitude that you are not of the world? And so again in company. Ah! beloved, believe me, company is one of the best tests for a Christian. You are invited to an evening party. Sundry amusements are provided which are not considered exactly sinful, but which certainly cannot come under the name of pious amusements. You sit there with the rest. There is a deal of idle chat going on, you would be thought puritanical to protest against it. Have you not come away—and notwithstanding all has been very pleasant, and friends have been very agreeable—have you not been inclined to say, "Ah! that does not do for me. I would rather be in a prayer meeting. I would rather be in an old broken down cow lodge with six old women, so long as I could be with the people of God, than in fine rooms with all the dainties and delicacies that could be provided without the company of Jesus. By God's grace I will seek to shun all these places as much as possible." That is a good test. You will prove in this way that you are not of the world. And you may do so in a great many other ways which I have no time to mention. Have you felt this experimentally, so that you can say, "I know that I am not of the world.

I feel it; I experience it." Don't talk of doctrine. Give me doctrine ground into experience. Doctrine is good, but experience is better. Experimental doctrine is the true doctrine which comforts and which edifies.

Practically

"They are not of the world, even as I am not of the world." And, first, allow me, man or woman, to apply this to you. *You who are of the world,* whose maxims, whose habits, whose behavior, whose feelings, whose everything is worldly and carnal, listen to this. Perhaps you make some profession of religion. Hear me, then. Your boasting of religion is empty as a phantom and shall pass away when the sun rises, as the ghosts sleep in their grave at the crowing of the cock. You have some pleasure in that professed religion of yours wherewith you are arrayed, and which you carry about you as a cloak and use as a stalking horse to your business, and a net to catch the honor in the world, and yet you are worldly like other men. Then I tell you if there be no distinction between yourself and the worldly, the doom of the worldly shall be your doom. If you were marked and watched, your next door tradesman would act as you do, and you act as he does. There is no distinction between you and the world. Hear me, then, it is God's solemn truth. You are none of His. If you are like the rest of the world, you are of the world. You are a goat and with goats you shall be cursed, for the sheep can always be distinguished from the goats by their appearance. O you worldly men of the world, you carnal professors, you who crowd our churches and fill our places of worship, this is God's truth! Let me say it solemnly. If I should say it as I ought, it would be weeping tears of blood. You are, with all your profession, "in the gall of bitterness" (Acts 8:23); with all your boastings, you are "in the bond of iniquity" (v. 23). For you act as others and shall come where others come, and it shall be done with you as with more notorious heirs of hell.

There is an old story which was once told of a dissenting minister. The old custom was that a minister might stop at an inn and not pay anything for his bed or his board. When he went to preach from place to place, he was charged nothing for the conveyance in which he rode. But on one occasion, a certain minister stopped at an inn and went to bed. The landlord listened and heard no prayer, so when he came down in the morning, he presented his bill. "Oh! I am not going to pay that, for I am a minister." "Ah!" said the landlord, "you went to bed last night like a sinner, and you shall pay this morning like a sinner. I will not let you go." Now, it strikes me that this will be the case with some of you when you come to God's bar. Though you pretended to be a Christian, you acted like a sinner, and you shall fare like a sinner too.

Your actions were unrighteous and were far from God. You shall have a portion with those whose character was the same as yours. "Be not deceived," it is easy to be so. "God is not mocked," though we often are, both minister and people. "God is not mocked: for whatsoever a man soweth, that shall he also reap" (Gal. 6:7).

And now we want to apply this to many *true children of God* who are here by way of caution. I say, my brother and sister Christian, you are not of the world. I am not going to speak hardly to you because you are my brother and sister, and in speaking to you I speak to myself also, for I am as guilty as you are. Have we not often been too much like the world? Do we not sometimes in our conversation talk too much like the world? Come, let me ask myself, are there not too many idle words that I say? Aye, that there are. And do I not sometimes give occasion to the enemy to blaspheme because I am not so different from the world as I ought to be? Come, let us confess our sins together. Have we not been too worldly? Ah! we have. Oh! let this solemn thought cross our minds: Suppose that after all we should not be His! For it is written, "Ye are not of the world." O God! if we are not right, make us so. Where we are a little right, make us still more right. And where we are wrong, amend us!

Allow me to tell a story to you. I told it when I was preaching last Tuesday morning, but it is worth telling again. There is a great evil in many of us being too light and frothy in our conversation. A very solemn thing once happened. A minister had been preaching in a country village, very earnestly and fervently. In the midst of his congregation there was a young man who was deeply impressed with a sense of sin under the sermon. He therefore sought the minister as he went out in hopes of walking home with him. They walked until they came to a friend's house. On the road the minister had talked about anything except the subject on which he had preached, though he had preached very earnestly, and even with tears in his eyes. The young man thought within himself, "Oh! I wish I could unburden my heart and speak to him, but I cannot. He does not say anything now about what he spoke of in the pulpit." When they were at supper that evening, the conversation was very far from what it should be, and the minister indulged in all kinds of jokes and light sayings. The young man had gone into the house with eyes filled with tears, feeling like a sinner should feel. But as soon as he got outside after the conversation, he stamped his foot and said, "It is a lie from beginning to end. That man has preached like an angel and now he has talked like a devil." Some years after the young man was taken ill and sent for this same minister. The minister did not know him. "Do you remember preaching at such-and-such a village?" asked the young man. "I do." "Your text was very deeply laid to my heart." "Thank God for that," said the minister. "Do not be so quick about thanking God," said the young man. "Do you know what you talked of that evening afterward when I went to supper with you? *Sir, I shall be damned!* And I will charge you before God's throne with being the author of my damnation. On that night I did feel my sin, but you were the means of scattering all my impressions." That is a solemn thought and teaches us how we should curb our tongues, especially those who are so lighthearted after solemn services and earnest preachings that we should not betray levity. Oh! let us take heed that we are not of the world, even as Christ was not of the world.

And Christian, lastly, by way of practice, let me comfort you with this. You are not of the world for your home is in heaven. Be content to be here a little for you are not of the world, and you shall go up to your own bright inheritance by-and-by. A man in traveling goes into an inn, and it is rather uncomfortable. "Well," says he, "I shall not have to stay here many nights. I have only to sleep here tonight. I shall be at home in the morning, so that I don't care much about one night's lodging being a little uncomfortable." So, Christian, this world is never a very comfortable one; but recollect, you are not of the world. This world is like an inn—you are only lodging here a little while. Put up with a little inconvenience because you are not of the world, even as Christ is not of the world. By-and-by, up yonder, you shall be gathered into your Father's house, and there you will find that there is a new heaven and a new earth provided for those who are "not of the world."

10

Believers Sent by Christ as Christ Is Sent by the Father

As thou hast sent me into the world, even so have I also sent them into the world (John 17:18).

Here is a great fact mentioned, namely, that the Father sent the Son into the world. In this our Lord's disciples had believed. Jesus says Himself, "They have believed that thou didst send me" (John 17:8). It is one of the first essentials of saving faith to believe in Christ as the sent one of God. They had proved, in their own experience, that Jesus was sent of God, for they had found Him to be sent to them. Especially they knew this because they had found in Him eternal life. To them it had been life eternal "to know the only true God, and Jesus Christ, whom He had sent." They had entered into the possession of a new and heavenly life, and they rejoiced therein, so that to them the fact that God had sent His Son into the world was indisputable. It was a fact upon which they based their salvation. It was their hope, their joy, their theme of thought, and subject of converse. They declared it with the accent of assurance.

Our Lord based upon that fact another. He says to His Father, "As thou hast sent me into the world, even so have I also sent them into the world." As surely as Christ was sent into the world by the Father, so surely are the saints sent into the world by Christ. Note well, that I say "the saints." I mean not the apostles only, but all the saints. I dare not limit the reference to what are called ordained ministers or apostles, for I believe it includes all the chosen of God. Was the prayer, contained in

This sermon was taken from *The Metropolitan Tabernacle Pulpit* and was preached on Sunday morning, January 22, 1882.

this seventeenth chapter of John, for the apostles only? I think not. Surely our Lord prayed for all whom the Father had given to Him and not for ministers only. Beyond question, our great Intercessor pleaded for all those whom the Father gave to Him. Hence it is of all these that He speaks in the words of our text. He mentions not only the officers, but the rank and file of the chosen host who have been called by grace to know Him as the sent of God. Be aye to them all, without exception, "As my Father hath sent me, even so send I you" (John 20:21). I do not for a moment dispute the need of a special call to the office of pastor or elder in the church of God, nor do I question that there are officers in the church of God upon whom peculiar responsibility rests. But no class of men may be exalted into a caste of Brahmins, who are alone sent into the world by the great Head of the church. We who spend our lives in teaching are your servants for Christ's sake, but we rejoice that you also have a high calling of God in Christ Jesus. If we have fuller knowledge of Scripture or larger gift of utterance, accept us as your fellow servants whose talents are cheerfully employed for your sakes. But if you have not these same talents, yet you have others, and you are equally given to Christ to be by Him sent into the world.

This is no trifle, but a very solemn business. To our Lord it was a special matter of prayer. It is here in that prayer which always seems to me to be the core of the whole Bible. Our Lord pleads not only about our being saved, but about our being sent. There is something here which deserves our deepest thought.

There are two petitions in our Lord's prayer which bear upon this. First, comes the petition—"Holy Father, keep them." You cannot serve God unless He preserves you. You will never keep the Lord's flock unless He first shepherds you. The Lord of the vineyard must keep the keepers, or their vineyards will not be kept. The other prayer immediately precedes the text: "Sanctify them." You cannot go out into the world as the sent ones of Christ unless you are sanctified. God will use no unholy messenger. You must be consecrated and cleansed, devoted and dedicated to God alone, or else you will not have the first qualification for the divine mission. Christ's prayer is, "Sanctify them through thy truth." The more truth you believe, the more sanctified you will be. The operation of truth upon the mind is to separate a man from the world to the service of God. Just in proportion as truth is given up, worldliness and frivolity are sure to prevail. A church which grows so enlightened as to neglect the doctrines of grace also falls in love with the vain amusements of the world. It has been so in all past ages, and it is sadly so today. But a church that, in a living way, holds fast the truth once for all delivered to the saints will also separate itself from the ways of the world. In fact, the world and the worldly church will shun it and push it into the place of separation. The more separated we are after our Master's fashion, the more fit shall we be to do His bidding.

Our Lord was evidently most careful as to our commission which He bases upon His own commission, and declares to be as certain and real as His own sending by the Father. He so valued this that He prays, "[Father], keep them" (John 17:15) and "[Father], sanctify them" (v. 17). May those two prayers be heard for us, and then we shall stand with our loins girt, our shoes on our feet, our lamps trimmed, and our lights burning, ready to go forth at the command of the Most High to the very ends of the earth. Our mission by Jesus grows out of His mission by the Father. We may learn much about it by considering how the Father sent the Son to be the Savior of the world.

Consider What Our Lord's Being Sent Involved to Himself

To a large extent, there will be a parallel between His being sent and ours. The parallel is drawn by way of quality, not of equality. Christ's commission is on a higher scale than ours. For He was sent to be a propitiation and covenant-head, and so came into positions which it would be presumption for us to dream of occupying. Still, there is a likeness, though it be only that of a drop to the sea.

Our Lord's mission involved *complete subjection to the Father's will*. He said, "My Father is greater than I" (John 14:28). This did not relate to His essential nature and dignity as God, but to the position which He took up in reference to the Father when He was sent to be our Savior. He that sends is greater than He that is sent. The Savior took up that subordinate position that He might do the Father's will. From that time forth, so long as He remained under His commission, He did not speak His own words nor do His own deeds. But He listened to the Father's will, and what the Father said to Him He both spoke and did. That is exactly where you and I have to place ourselves now, deliberately and unreservedly. Our Lord sends us, and we are to be, in very deed, subordinate to His command in all things. We are no longer masters; we have become servants. Our will is lost in the will of our glorious Superior. If we are ambitious and our ambition is guided by wisdom, it will take us down to that basin and the towel, and we shall be willing to wash the disciples' feet to show that we are sent by our condescending Lord. We shall henceforth have no respect to our own dignity or interest but shall lay ourselves out to serve Him to whom we belong. Whatsoever He says to us we shall aim to do. Although we are sons of God, yet we are also servants. We would not do our own will but the will of Him that sent us. Oh, to be sound on this point so as to yield our members in perfect obedience, and even bring every thought into subjection to Christ! Oh, to die to self and live in Christ! Can you drink of this cup, and be baptized with this baptism? I trust you can. If so, you shall fulfill the errand upon which He sends you.

This meant for our Lord *the quitting of His rest*. He reigned in heaven, and all angels paid Him homage. But when the Father sent Him, He left His high abode. He was laid in the manger, for there was no room for Him in the inn. Where the horned oxen fed, there must the holy child be cradled. The royalties of heaven are left behind. The rest which He enjoyed in the bosom of the Father must be renounced for toil, hunger, thirst, weariness, and the death at the cross. Dear friends, you may serve the Lord, and yet be as happy as your Lord was. But if Jesus has sent you into the world you are not to seek ease or comfort. You are not even to make your own spiritual comfort the first object of your thought. How nice that evening at home would be! But you are sent, and therefore must turn out to win souls. How delightful it would be to read that book through, and to leave the class alone! But you must not, for you are sent to instruct and save. Henceforth you are to consider nothing but how you can answer the design of Him who has sent you. Your aim must be to do the utmost possible for your Lord. The Christian who does much is still an idler if he could do more. We have never reached the point of diligence until we are doing all that lies in us and are even then wishing to do far more. Bought with His precious blood, the vows of the Lord are upon us, and we renounce our natural love of ease that we may please Him who has sent us.

When sent of God, the Savior also had *to forego even heaven itself.* He was here on earth the God-man, the Mediator, and He did not return to the splendor of His Father's court until He could say, "I have finished the work which thou gavest me to do. And now, O Father, glorify thou me" (John 17:4–5). We must not sigh for heaven while so much is to be done on earth. The rest of glory will come soon, but just now we have to do with the work of grace. Let us stick to our work here below and do it thoroughly well, for our Lord has gone above and is preparing a place for us. Is it not wonderful how God even now denies Himself for the salvation of men? Why does not our Lord come at once in His glory? Why do we not see the millennial reign begin? It is because of the long-suffering of God. He waits and puts off the closing scene because He is "not willing that any should perish, but that all should come to repentance." He keeps back even the glorious advent to give men space for salvation. That for which Jesus longs and the Spirit longs and the spouse longs is kept back in mercy to the guilty. The Bridegroom postpones His marriage day that men may be brought to Him by the divine long-suffering. If Jesus can do this, surely we may well wait out of compassion to our fellowmen. Even our hope of being forever with the Lord may wait awhile. So long as there is another sinner for us to rescue, we will remain in this land of our exile. That is what our Lord means: The Father has sent Me from heaven and kept Me out of heaven, for the sake of men. Even so shall I detain you among the tents of Kedar for awhile that you may bring in My redeemed through the Gospel.

The words of our text are, "As thou hast sent me *into the world.*" This implies *affinity with men.* Our Lord was not sent to the edge of the world to look over the fence and converse hopefully from a distance, but He was sent right into the world. He took on Him human nature and became bone of our bone. We read, "Then drew near unto him all the publicans and sinners for to hear him" (Luke 15:1). He was a man among men. In this way Jesus has sent you, my friends, into families, into offices, into establishments, into places where you labor for daily bread among a company of ungodly men. Do not cry out because you have thus to mingle with them. Your Lord was sent into the world, not, I say, to the outskirts of it nor to some elevated mountain high above it from which He might look down. He was sent into the world in an emphatic sense. So are you sent, wisely sent, to tarry even among unconverted, infidel, and impure men that you may do for Christ His great work and make known His salvation.

He was sent into the world, and this involved abiding in humiliation. "The world knew him not" (John 1:10), therefore the world knows us not because it knew Him not. You are not sent into the world to be honored and pampered, nor even to receive your righteous due. If God aimed at your immediate glorification, He would take you to heaven. But He aims at your humiliation that you may be like His Firstborn. You are to have fellowship with the Only-begotten in many ways; and among the rest, you are to be partakers of His sufferings. Expect to be misunderstood, misrepresented, belied, ridiculed, and so forth, for so was the Sent of the Father. You are to look for evil treatment. For as the Father sent His Son into a world which was sure to treat him ill, so has He sent you into the same world which will treat you in the same manner if you are like your Lord. Be not surprised at persecution, but look for it and take it as part of the covenant entail. For as Ishmael mocked Isaac, so will the seed after the flesh persecute that which is born according to promise.

In a word, your being sent of Christ involves *unreserved dedication to His work.* When Christ came into the world He did nothing but what His Father sent Him to do. He had no secondary object of any sort. From the reservoir of His being, no little stream trickled away in waste, but the whole of it went to turn the great mill-wheel of His life. The whole current and force of His nature went in one way, working out one design. Now, as the Father sent Jesus, so has Jesus sent you to be henceforth by occupation a Christian. You are to be consecrated wholly and alone to the one object for which Christ has set you apart. There may be other lawful objects, but these you render subsidiary to the one object of your life. You have but one eye, and that eye looks to your Lord. Henceforth you belong to Christ, body, soul, and spirit—from the morning light to the evening shade and through the night watches. There is not a hair of your head but what Jesus values, for He has put it down in the inventory—"the very hairs of your head are all numbered" (Matt. 10:30). Give him, then, every single power, however feeble; every part of your nature, however insignificant. Let your whole being be the Lord's, for "ye are not your own. For ye are bought with a price" (1 Cor. 6:19–20). "This is a high standard," says one. My friends, it is none too high. It is sad that any should think it so. God help you to know that you are sent and clearly to perceive what your mission involves. We, too, are missioned from above. We, too, are to have a hand in the saving of the world.

Consider Why Our Lord Was Sent into the World

Our Lord came here with one design. Christ was not sent to teach a correct system of philosophy. He was not Plato, but Jesus; not a sage, but a Savior. He could have solved the problems of the universe, but He did not even allude to them. He was not an Aristotle ruling the world of human thought, although He could have done so easily had He chosen. Blessed be His name, He came to save from sin. This no Plato or Aristotle could have done. All the sages and philosophers put together are not worth so much as the little finger of a Christ. Christ entered into no rivalry with the academy. He came on a very different errand. Neither was our Lord sent to be an inventor or a discoverer. All the discoveries that have been made in modern times could have been at once revealed by Him. But that was not His object, and He kept scrupulously to His one design. He could have told us the secret of the Dark Continent, but He was not sent for that end. He could have anticipated all that we have slowly learned and saved the world the long processes of experiment and observation, but this was not the object of His mission.

He did not come to be a conqueror. God gave us in Him neither Alexander nor Caesar—of such slaughterers the world has always had enough and to spare. He conquers evil, but not by the sword. Our Lord did not come even to be a politician, a reformer of governments, a rectifier of social economics. There came one to Him who said, "Master, speak to my brother, that he divide the inheritance with me" (Luke 12:13). You might have supposed that the Lord would have arbitrated in that case. But He did not do so, for He said, "Who made me a judge or a divider over you?" (Luke 12:14). He kept to His one business, and we shall be wise to do the same. Point me to a single instance in which He interfered with the government of Pilate or of Herod. Had He anything to say about the tyranny of Caesar? When He takes Caesar's penny in His hand, He simply says, "Render therefore unto Caesar the things which are Caesar's, and unto God the things that are God's" (Matt. 22:21). He was none of Caesar's, for He belonged to God and to God alone.

Should not Christian people take heed that they follow Christ in this unity of aim and purpose? This I know, I am not sent to preach to you any new philosophical system, nor to advocate any political party, nor to meddle with any of those social matters that can be better managed by others. It is mine to preach the Gospel of the grace of God, and this one thing I do. If you can serve Christ and your fellowmen in any way, do it. But never get away from your one aim and purpose. If we are enabled to save men's souls by the Holy Spirit resting upon our teaching we may die content, even though we have left fifty other excellent things undone. There are enough of the dead to bury the dead. Burying the dead is a good work, but this will be a labor more congenial to the dead around us than to ourselves. Let us leave it to them. We cannot do everything. Let us do that which we are sent to do.

Oh, that every Christian would feel that, whatever else he would like to be, his first business is to be a servant of Christ. Your first concern is to serve Christ, and it ought to be your second thing to serve Christ. Then I would claim that it should be your third thing, and I shall get far on in numbers before I should allow any other character to take a leading position. May no possible object bear any comparison in your desires and endeavors in comparison with your resolve to glorify God your Savior!

Notice, further, that *our Lord was not sent to be ministered unto, but to minister.* I fear that many of His professed servants think they have been sent to be ministered to. Their religion consists in coming to places of worship to be ministered to. Through the week they would like to have very particular attention from the pastor and the church officers, and you hear them grumbling that they are not sufficiently looked after. Surely, they must have been sent, not to minister, but to be ministered to. Friends, let us give them as much as we can of our services, for they evidently need them. But Jesus was not sent to be visited and waited on and served. He came to minister to others. He did so to the full and could truly say, "I am among you as he that serveth" (Luke 22:27). Beloved friend, you know that it is more blessed to give than to receive. Therefore feel it to be your joy to live as one who is sent by Jesus to be the servant of the church and the winner of souls.

Let us inquire what was Christ's work upon earth. It was, first, *to teach.* Wherever He went He was an instructor of the ignorant. He preached of the kingdom, of faith, and of grace. We are to teach. "I do not know anything," says one. Then do not tell it, but first go to the Lord and ask Him to teach you something. As soon as ever you know the A B C of the Gospel, go and teach somebody that A B C. You need not teach him D E F and G H I until you have advanced so far yourself, but teach all you are taught. Learn first; but when you have learned, then let others learn from you. This is what Jesus did. We need to be teaching the Gospel everywhere.

Forget not that *He lived,* and His living was teaching. His actions were so many heads of His life sermon. His every movement was instructive. He went about doing good. Make your life tally with your teaching, and make your life to be a part of your teaching—no, the best part of your discourse. The most solid and most emphatic teaching that comes from you should be what you do rather than what you say. Christ has sent you into the world for that end.

Our Lord came also *to suffer for the cause of truth and righteousness.* If you follow Him closely, you must expect to suffer also. Do not cry out about it as though some strange thing had happened to you. Take joyfully the spoiling of your good name. If Christ has sent you forth like sheep in the midst of wolves, wonder not that the wolf gives you a bite or two. Is it not his nature? Let the wolf howl, but do not trouble yourself about it. What else should a wolf do? When pain, weakness, and bodily infirmity seize on you, and you lie for days and weeks tossed with pain all through the sleepless nights, take it all patiently and say, "I am sent to show patience, that men may see what grace can do."

You are sent *to save men.* It is true that you have not to redeem them by blood, *that* the Lord has done most effectually. You have not to suffer as a substitute, for His one sacrifice has sufficed. But you are sent to seek and to save that which was lost by proclaiming salvation by Christ Jesus. Every man who is saved himself should feel that he is called at once to labor for the salvation of others. Your election is not only election to personal salvation, but to personal service. You are chosen that, through your being saved, others may be called into the like felicity. View this very clearly and get it fixed in your minds, and then carry it out in your daily lives.

"Ah!" say you, "our Lord might very well give Himself up to His work, for if He had not done so the whole world must have perished." Listen! *Your work also is indispensable.* How is the work of Christ to be made effectual among the sons of men for their salvation? Must they not hear it that they may believe it? How shall they hear without a preacher? I venture to say that as the salvation of men depended upon

Christ, so, in another sense, the salvation of men at this hour depends upon the church of God. If believers do not go and preach Christ, who will? If you that love Him do not commend Him, who will? Do you think that the Houses of Parliament will ever meet together to consider the evangelization of the heathen? If the government did take such work in hand, it could do nothing, for it is not a fit agent and would hinder rather than help the good design. Do you think the worldlings, the skeptics, the critics will ever unite to spread the kingdom of Christ and save the souls of men? Do not dream it. If the church of God does not go forth on her holy errand, nothing will be done. "But it might be done by angels," says one. I know it might, but "unto the angels hath he not put in subjection the world to come, whereof we speak" (Heb. 2:5). He has committed to us the word of reconciliation, even to us who are men. We must attend to it or great guilt will be upon us.

I should like every Christian to feel that he has to be the instrument of salvation to certain persons. It is all allotted. The whole country is measured and divided, and we have each our portion which we must conquer for our Lord. If I belong to the tribe of Judah, I have to help my brothers and sisters to drive out the Canaanites from our portion. If you belong to the tribe of Issachar or Benjamin, you must look to your own allotment and clear it of the enemy. Joshua is the leader, but every Israelite is in his army. Christ has power over all flesh as the head of the body. He has given to each of His members a portion of His power, so that each member of His body has power over some portion of "all flesh." That power must be used in the giving of eternal life to as many as the Father has given to Jesus. God grant that you may feel this and may go to your work as Christ went to His!

Consider How Our Lord Came

First, our Lord came *with alacrity*. The work of our Redeemer was no forced work. He was sent, but He willingly came.

> Down from the shining seats above
> With joyful haste he fled.

"Lo, I come to do thy will, O God," said He. He came cheerfully among the sons of men. You that are sent of Christ must always go gladly to your service. Never look as if you were driven to the field like oxen which love not the plow. God does not delight in a slavish spirit. If we serve Christ because of the yoke of duty, we shall serve badly. But when our service is our pleasure, when we thank God that to us is this grace given that we should "preach among the Gentiles the unsearchable riches of Christ" (Eph. 3:8), then we shall labor wisely, zealously, and acceptably.

Next, our Lord came *with authority*. The Lord God had sent Him.

He had the Father at His back. Be sure that, when Jesus sends you, you are invested with authority, and they that despise you do it at their peril. Your blunders and mistakes are not authorized. But so far as you speak His Word with a desire for His glory, He that receives you receives Christ, even as our Lord said, "He that receiveth me receiveth him that sent me" (Matt. 10:40). God is with you, be not afraid. Your Lord will not let your words fall to the ground.

Our Lord came *with ability,* too. What did His ability consist in? Mainly in this—"The Spirit of the Lord is upon me, because he hath anointed me" (Luke 4:18). This is also where your sufficiency must be found, and you can have as much as you please of it. You cannot get every faculty of the brain, but you can have every influence of the Spirit. It may be you cannot reach the highest form of education or of utterance, but these things are not vital. God can speak by your stammering tongue, even as in the case of Moses. You shall do the Lord's work, and do it well, if you are anointed of the Holy Spirit. He who does Christ's work in Christ's power works an abiding work which will eternally glorify God. He who sends us out into the world to carry the Gospel to every creature will give us grace to obey His bidding.

Our Lord came *with absorption.* Jesus came, as I have said before, to do what He was sent to do and nothing else. He meddled with nothing beyond His vocation. Every thought of His manhood, every power of His Godhead, He devoted to fulfilling the errand on which He came. His zeal had eaten Him up. He was covered with it as with a cloak. The man Christ was all on fire, and all on fire with one desire, that He might finish the work that His Father had given Him to do. For this joy He endured the cross, despising the shame.

Our Lord came *with abiding resolve* to go through with His mission to the end. He never thought of going back. He steadfastly set His face to go to Jerusalem. He pressed through shame, through death to accomplish our redemption. In these days we shall not do much unless we have a desperate determination to persevere in the teeth of difficulties. Those who can go back will go back. Remember how Gideon proclaimed throughout the host that if any man was fainthearted he might go home. So do we proclaim today: go home if you are wavering. If you do not love Christ enough to be resolved to serve Him to the last, what is the good of you? You will break down and lose us the victory at some important crisis. He that has been bought with the blood of Christ and knows it, feels that he must endure to the end, for only he that endures to the end shall be saved. We go because our Lord's sending constrains us. "Woe is unto me, if I preach not the gospel!" (1 Cor. 9:16). Woe is to you if you do not teach the children or speak to individuals or write letters or in some way fulfill your mission!

Consider How Our Lord Behaved as the Sent One

Our Lord *began early*. While He was yet a youth He said, "Wist ye not that I must be about my Father's business?" (Luke 2:49). As soon as ever a man is converted, he should inquire, "Lord, what wilt thou have me to do?" (Acts 9:6). Young believer, do not let many weeks pass over your head before you have attempted somewhat for your Lord. I will correct that exhortation. I wish you would not let a single day pass away without your bearing testimony for your Master.

But, next, our *Lord waited very patiently*. He was thirty years old before He preached openly. We do not know all that He did in the workshop at Nazareth. Is it not possible that He supported His widowed mother by His hand-labor? We do not know. But of this we are sure, that it is the duty of many young men to look after their parents first. It is the duty of all to "show piety at home." Many Christian women will have done well if they have carried out home duties. She was a holy woman upon whose grave they placed this epitaph, "She made home happy." This is what Jesus did for the first thirty years of His life. He was doing the Father's will when He was a young man at home. Though He did not preach, yet while He was working and learning He was carrying out the purpose for which He was sent.

When the time came for Him to commence His more public service, *He sought proper entrance* into it. He did not blunder into God's work by a rush and a leap, but He went to John to be baptized and to be publicly recognized as the Messiah. John was the porter, and he opened the gate to the Good Shepherd, who came in by the door and did not climb up some other way. He came to John, who represented the prophetic chair of the Jewish church, and so He entered into His work as minister in a lawful and proper way. I like our young friends, when they feel their time has come for public service, to begin in right style and due order, carrying out the Lord's mind in the Lord's way. Willfulness in beginning may throw a man out of gear as to his future work. It argues a spirit ill prepared for acceptable service.

That being passed, see *how He labored at His work*. He was always doing the Father's will. He worked all the day, every day, everywhere, with everybody. Some Christian people can only render occasional service. They are very good at a convention. They save up their holiness for meetings. At a religious gathering they are in fine form, but they are not everyday saints. The kind of person the church needs most is the maid-of-all-work, the worker who can turn his hand to anything that providence allots him and is glad to do so, however humbling it may be. My venerated grandmother owned a set of choice china which is, I believe part of it, in existence now. Why does it exist now? It has seen little service. It only came out on high-days and holidays—say once in six months when ministers and friends came to tea. It was a very nice set of old china—too good for children to break. Some Christians are like that fine old ware: it would not do to use them too often. They are too good for every day. They do not teach their servants and try to win the poor people in their own neighborhood to Christ. But they talk well at a conference. Oh, you fine bits of egg-shell china, I know you! Don't fear. I am not going to break you. Yet I would somewhat trouble you by the remark that in the case of such ware as you are, more pieces get broken in the cupboard than on the table. You will last all the longer if you get to work for Christ in everyday work. Jesus was not sent out for particular occasions, and neither are you. We use our Lord for a thousand hallowed purposes, and even so will He use us from time to time, if we are but ready and willing.

Notice about our Lord's service that *His prayers always kept pace with His work.* This is where most of us fail. When our Lord had a long day's work, we find Him taking a long night's prayer. "I have so much to do," says one, "that I could not be long in prayer." That is putting the case the wrong way upward. When you have most to do, you have most need to pray. Unless you keep up the proportion, your offering will fail in quality. The holy incense was sweet before God because in that sacred compound there was a proportion of each spice. So in our lives there must be a due measure of Word and work and prayer and praise. I may say of prayer what one said of salt in the Scripture, "Salt without prescribing how much" (Ezra 7:22). Prayer can never be in excess. You can salt meat too much, but you cannot salt your service too much with prayer. If you are accustomed to pray in your walk and works, at all hours and seasons, you do not err. There never will be in any of us a superfluity of devotion. God help you to be like His Son who, though He was sent and had the Father with Him, yet could not live without prayer. No you not only feel your need of prayer, but fill up that need abundantly!

Once more, in all that Jesus did *He remained in constant fellowship with the Father.* He said, "He that sent me is with me" (John 8:29). That is a beautiful sentence. Let me repeat it—"He that sent me is with me." The great Father had never to call to Jesus and say, "Come nearer. You are departing from Me. You are too busy with Mary and Lazarus and Peter and John, and so you are forgetting Me." No, no. He did always the things that pleased God, and He was always in communion with the great Father in everything that He did. "Ah!" says one, "it is hard to commune with God and be very busy." Yes, but it will prove harder still to have been very busy and not to have dwelt with God. It is easy to do much when you walk with God, and easier still to make a great fuss and do nothing because the Lord is away. To get near omnipotence will not make you omnipotent, but it will make you feel omnipotence working with you. Oh, that we might thus dwell with God as Jesus did, for He has sent us for this even as the Father sent Him.

I would leave with you four words. We are sent; therefore, whenever we try to press Christ upon men *we are not guilty of intrusion.* We have sometimes known strangers to be asked in this place about their souls by certain of our friends, and they have grown angry at such a question. This is very silly of them, is it not? But I hope the friend who meets with an angry answer will not be at all hurt. You are not intrusive, though the angry person says you are. You are sent, and where Jesus sends you, you have a right to go. The postman frequently knocks at the door as late as ten o'clock. I suppose you want to be asleep. Do you cry out—"How dare you make that noise?" No, he is the postman, an officer of Her Majesty, and he is sent out with the last mail and must deliver the letters. You cannot blame him for doing that for which he is sent. Go you and knock at the doors of the careless and the sleepy. Give them a startling word. Do not let them perish for want of a warning or an invitation. Go on without fear; your commission is your warrant. If Jesus has sent you, you have a right to speak even to princes and kings.

Next, we are sent; therefore, *we dare not run away.* If Jesus bids us go forward, we must not retreat. If what we have preached and taught be of God, if we are ridiculed for it, let us take no notice, but steam ahead. Put more coals in the furnace, get the steam up, and go faster than ever in the same course. We defy the Devil to stop us, for we are sent.

Next, we are sent; therefore, *we are sure to be helped.* Our King never sends a servant on an errand at his own charges. *Our* own power fails us, but He never allows His power to fail us when engaged in His service. Those who are sent shall be sustained.

But, if we are sent, remember lastly, *we have to give an account.* Our Lord does not call for the time sheet every night, but a time sheet is kept all the same. There will be a day for passing in the checks, and we shall have to answer for what we have done. I speak not now to you ungodly ones, whose account will be terrible at that last great day. God save you! May you believe on Him whom God has sent! But now I speak to Christian people. You will have to render your account, and may God grant you may not have to make a lamentable return in this fashion—"On such a day so much wood, and on such a day so much hay, and on such a day so much stubble." Let there be down in your book nothing but gold, silver, and precious stones, for it must all be tried with fire. If you yourself are saved and your work is burned up, you will suffer loss. What pain to find your lifework to be a lot of wood, hay, and stubble which will blaze furiously and die out in ashes! You know what I mean—so much time spent in planning frivolous amusements for the people, so much talent expended in teaching what is not the Gospel, so much zeal consumed upon matters which do not concern eternal things, all this will burn. Beloved, do your Master's work, win souls, preach Christ, expound your Bibles, pray men to be reconciled to God, plead with men to come to Christ. This kind of work will stand the fire. When the last great day shall dawn, this will remain to glory and honor. God bless you for Christ's sake!

11

"I Will"; Yet, "Not as I Will"

Father, I will (John 17:24)
Not as I will (Matthew 26:39).

W e have here two prayers uttered by the same Person. Yet there is the greatest possible contrast between them. How different men are at different times! Yet Jesus was always essentially the same: "the same yesterday, and today, and for ever" (Heb. 13:8). Still, His mood and state of mind varied from time to time. He seemed calmly happy when He prayed with His disciples and said, "Father, I will that they also, whom thou hast given me, be with me where I am; that they may behold my glory, which thou hast given me" (John 17:24). But He was in agony when in Gethsemane, having withdrawn from His disciples and fallen on His face, He prayed saying, "O my Father, if it ho possible, let this cup pass from me: nevertheless not as I will, but as thou wilt" (Matt. 26:39). It is the same Man, and an unchangeable Man, too, as to His essence, who uttered both prayers. Yet see how different were His frames of mind, and how different the prayers He offered.

Brother, you may be the same man, and quite as good a man, when you are groaning before God as when you are singing before him. There may be more grace even in the submissive "Not as I will" than in the triumphant "Father, I will." Do not judge yourselves to have changed in your standing before God because you have undergone an alteration as to your feelings. If your Master prayed so differently at different times, you, who have not the fullness of grace that He had, must not wonder if you have a great variety of inward experiences.

Notice, also, that it was not only the same Person, but that He used these two expressions almost at the same time. I do not know how

---

This sermon was taken from *The Metropolitan Tabernacle Pulpit* and was preached on Sunday evening, July 1, 1888.

many minutes—I had better say minutes rather than hours—intervened between the last supper, and the wonderful high-priestly prayer, and the agonizing cries of Gethsemane. I suppose that it was only a short walk from Jerusalem to the olive garden, and that it would not occupy long to traverse the distance. At one end of the walk Jesus prays, "Father, I will"; at the other end of it, he says, "Not as I will." In like manner, we may undergo great changes and have to alter the tone of our prayers in a few minutes. You prayed just now with holy confidence. You took firm hold of the covenant angel and with wrestling Jacob you said, "I will not let thee go, except thou bless me" (Gen. 32:26). Yet it may be equally becoming on your part within an hour to lie in the very dust and in agony to cry to the Lord, "Pardon my prayers. Forgive me that I was too bold, and hear me now as I cry to You and say, 'Not as I will, but as thou wilt.'"

> If but my fainting heart he blest
> With thy sweet Spirit for its guest,
> My God, to thee I leave the rest;
> "Thy will be done!"

Never be ashamed because you have to mend your prayers. Be careful not to make a mistake if you can help it. But, if you make one, do not be ashamed to confess it and to correct it as far as you can. One of our frequent mistakes is that we wonder that we make mistakes. Whenever a man says, "I should never have thought that I could have done such a foolish thing as that," it shows that he did not really know himself. For had he known himself, he would rather have wondered that he did not do worse. He would have marveled that he acted as wisely as he did. Only the grace of God can teach us how to run our prayers down the scale from the high note of "Father, hear me, for You have said, 'Ask what thou wilt,'" right down to the deep, deep bass of "Father . . . not as I will, but as thou wilt."

I must further remark that these two prayers were equally characteristic of Christ. I think that I should know my Lord by His voice in either of them. Who but the eternal Son of God may dare to say, "Father, I will"? There speaks Incarnate Deity; that is the sublime utterance of the well-beloved Son. And yet who could say as He said it, "If it be possible, let this cup pass from me: nevertheless not as I will, but as thou wilt"? Perhaps you have uttered those words, dear friend. But in your case they were not concerning such a cup of woe as Christ emptied. There were but a few drops of gall in your cup. His was all bitterness from the froth to the dregs—all bitterness, and such bitterness as, thank God, you and I can never taste! That cup He has drained to the dregs, and we shall not have to drink one drop from it. But it was of that cup that He said—and I detect the voice of the Son of God, the Son of man, in that brief utterance—"Not as I will, but as thou wilt."

My two texts make up a strange piece of music. Blessed are the lips that know how to express the confidence that rises to the height as far as we can go with Christ, and descends even to the deeps as far as we can go with Him in full submission to the will of God. Does anybody say that he cannot understand the contrast between these two prayers? Dear friend, it is to be explained thus. There was a difference of position in the Suppliant on these two occasions. The first prayer, "Father, I will," is the prayer of our great High Priest with all His heavenly garments on—the blue and purple and fine twined linen, the pomegranates, the golden bells, and the breastplate with the twelve precious stones bearing the names of His chosen people. It is our great High Priest, in the glory of His majestic office and power, who says to God, "Father, I will." The second Suppliant is not so much the Priest as the Victim. Our Lord is there seen bound to the altar, about to feel the sacrificial knife, about to be consumed with the sacrificial fire. You hear Him as though it were a lamb bleating, and the utterance is, "Not as I will, but as thou wilt." The first petition is the language of Christ in power pleading for us. The second is the utterance of Christ made sin for us that we might be made the righteousness of God in Him. That is the difference of position that explains the contrast in the prayers.

Let me tell you also that there is a difference in the subject of His supplication, which is full of instruction. In the first prayer where our Lord says so majestically, "Father, I will," He is pleading for His people, praying for what He knows to be the Father's will, officiating there before God as the very mouthpiece of God, and speaking of something about which He is perfectly clear and certain. When you are praying for God's people, you may pray very boldly. When you are pleading for God's cause, you may speak very positively. When you know you are asking what is definitely promised in the Scriptures as part of the covenant ordered in all things and sure, you may ask without hesitation as our Lord did. But, in the second case, Jesus was praying for Himself: "If it be possible, let this cup pass from me." He was praying about a matter concerning which He did not, as man, know the Father's will, for He says, "If it be possible." There is an "if" in it: "If it be possible, let this cup pass from me." Whenever you go upstairs in an agony of distress and begin to pray about yourself and about a possible escape from suffering, always say under such circumstances, "Nevertheless not as I will, but as thou wilt." It may be given you sometimes to pray very boldly even in such a case as that. But, if it is not given you, take care that you do not presume. I may pray for healing for my body, but not with such confidence as I pray for the prosperity of Zion and the glory of God. That which has to do with myself I may ask as a child of God asks of his Father; but I must ask submissively, leaving the decision wholly in his hands, feeling that, because it is for myself rather than for him, I must say, "Nevertheless not as I will, but as thou wilt." I think that there is a plain lesson here for Christians to take heed that, while they are very confident on one subject for which they pray, they are equally submissive on another. For there is a heavenly blending in the Christian character, as there was in Christ's character, a firm confidence and yet an absolute yielding to the will of God, let that will be what it may.

> Lord, my times are in thy hand;
> All my sanguine hopes have plann'd
> To thy wisdom I resign,
> And would make thy purpose mine.

Now all this while you may say that I have only been going around the text. Very well; but, sometimes, there is a good deal of instruction to be picked up around a text. The manna fell around the camp of Israel. Peradventure there is some manna around this text. May the Lord help every one of us to gather His portion!

I want you now, for a few minutes, to view this great Suppliant in the two moods in which He prayed, "Father, I will," and "Not as I will," and then to combine the two. We will, first, view *Jesus in the power of His intercession.* Next, we will talk of *Jesus in the power of His submission.* In the third place, we will try to *combine the two prayers*, "I will"; yet, "Not as I will."

Jesus in the Power of His Intercession

Whence did He derive that power? Who enabled Him thus to speak with God and say, "Father, I will"? First, *Jesus prayed in the power of His Sonship.* Sons may say to their fathers what strangers may not dare to say. Such a Son was Jesus—so near to His Father's heart. He was a Son who could say, "The Father hath not left me alone; for I do always those things that please him" (John 8:29). Jesus was also One of whom the Father had said, "This is my beloved Son, in whom I am well pleased" (Matt. 3:17). Well might He have power with God so as to be able to say, "Father, I will."

Next, He derived this power from *the Father's eternal love to Him.* Did you notice how, in the very verse from which our text is taken, Jesus says to his Father, "Thou lovedst me before the foundation of the world"? We cannot conceive what the love of the Father is to Christ Jesus His Son. Remember, they are one in essence. God is one— Father, Son, and Holy Spirit. As the Incarnate God, Christ is unspeakably dear to the Father's heart. There is nothing about Him of which the Father disapproves. There is nothing lacking in Him that the Father would desire to see there. He is God's ideal of Himself: "In him dwelleth all the fulness of the Godhead bodily" (Col. 2:9). Well may one who is the subject of His Father's eternal love be able to say, "Father, I will."

But *our Lord Jesus also based this prayer upon His finished work.* I grant you that He had not yet actually died, but in the certain prospect of His doing so He had said to His Father, "I have glorified thee on the earth: I have finished the work which thou gavest me to do" (John 17:4). Now He has actually finished it. He has been able in the fullest sense to say, "It is finished" (John 19:30), and He has gone up to take His place in glory at His Father's side. You remember the argument with which Paul begins his Epistle to the Hebrews: "God, who at sundry times and in divers manners spake in time past unto the fathers by the prophets, hath in these last days spoken unto us by his Son, whom he hath appointed heir of all things, by whom also he made the worlds; who being the brightness of his glory, and the express image of his person, and upholding all things by the word of his power, when he had by himself purged our sins, sat down on the right hand of the Majesty on high; being made so much better than the angels, as he hath by inheritance obtained a more excellent name than they. For unto which of the angels said he at any time, Thou art my Son, this day have I begotten thee? And again, I will be to him a Father, and he shall be to me a Son?" (1:1–5). When the Father looks at Christ, He sees in Him atonement accomplished, satisfaction presented, sin annihilated, the elect redeemed, the covenant ratified, the everlasting purpose settled on eternal foundations. O beloved, since Christ has magnified God's law and made it honorable, and since He has poured out His soul to death, He may well possess the power to say, "Father, I will."

Remember, too, that *Jesus still possesses this power,* and possesses it for you and for me. O my dear hearers, you may well go to Christ and accept Him as your Mediator and Intercessor since all this power to say, "Father, I will," is laid up in Him on purpose for poor believing sinners who come and take Him to be their Savior! You say that you cannot pray. Well, He can. Ask Him to plead for you. I thank God that, sometimes, when we do not ask Him to plead for us, He does it all the same as He did for Peter when Satan had desired to have Him, but Christ had prayed for him. Peter did not know his danger. But the Savior did, and He pleaded for him at once. What a blessing it is to think of Christ, clothed with divine authority and power, using it all for us! Well does Toplady sing—

With cries and tears he offer'd up
His humble suit below;
But with authority he asks,
Enthroned in glory now.

For all that come to God by him,
Salvation he demands;
Points to their names upon his breast,
And spreads his wounded hands.

His covenant and sacrifice
Give sanction to his claim;
"Father, I will that all my saints
Be with me where I am."

Further, *that power of Christ will land every believer in heaven.*
Notice how Christ turns all His pleading with God that way. He says,
"Father, I will, that they also, whom thou hast given me, be with me
where I am; that they may behold my glory." The Devil says that we
shall never get to heaven. But we remember that declaration of Moses,
"Thine enemies shall be found liars unto thee" (Deut. 33:29). The archenemy will be found to be the archliar, for the Lord's prayer will be
heard. As He pleads that those whom the Father gave Him should be
brought up to be with Him where He is, you may depend upon it that
they will all arrive safely in heaven. And you, if you are among those
who are given to Christ—and you may know that by your faith in
Him—shall be among that blessed company.

I shall have finished with this first point when I have said this, *that
power which Christ had may, in a measure, be gained by all His
people.* I dare not say, and I would not say, that any one of us will ever
be able to utter our Savior's words, "Father, I will." But I do say this, if
you abide in Christ, and His words abide in you, you may attain to such
power in prayer that you shall ask what you will, and it shall be done to
you. This is not a promise to all of you—no, not even to all of you who
are God's people—but only to those of you who live wholly to God and
serve Him with all your heart. You can, by an established relationship
with God, attain to such power with the Most High that men shall say
of you what they used to say of Luther, "There goes a man who can ask
what he likes of God and have it." You may attain to that glorious alti-
tude. Oh, I would that every one of us would seek to reach this height
of power and blessing! It is not the feeble Christian or the worldly
Christian who has just enough grace to make him miserable, or enough
grace to keep him from being absolutely immoral, that is not the man
who will prevail with God. You paddlers in Christianity who scarcely
wet your toes, you who never go in beyond your ankles or your knees,

God will never give you this privilege unless you go in for it. Get where the waters are deep enough to swim in and plunge in. Be perfectly consecrated to God. Yield your whole lives to His glory without reserve. Then may you obtain something of your Master's power in prayer when He said, "Father, I will."

Jesus in the Power of His Submission

Our second text is all submission: "Not as I will." This utterance, "Not as I will," proved that the shrinkings of Christ's nature from that dreadful cup were all overcome. I do not believe that Christ was afraid to die. Do you believe that? Oh, no; many of His servants have laughed at death. I am sure that He was not afraid to die. What was it, then, that made that cup so awfully terrible? Jesus was to be made sin for us. He was to come under the curse for us. He was to feel the Father's wrath on account of human guilt. His whole nature, not alone His flesh, but His whole being shrank from that fearful ordeal. It was not actual defilement that was to come upon Him, but it looked like it. As man He could not tell what that cup of wrath must contain.

> Immanuel, sunk with dreadful woe,
> Unfelt, unknown to all below—
> Except the Son of God
> In agonizing pangs of soul,
> Drinks deep of wormwood's bitterest bowl,
> And sweats great drops of blood.

After dwelling in the love of God from all eternity, He was in a few hours to bear the punishment of man's sin. Yet He must bear it, and therefore He said, "Not as I will, but as thou wilt." Do you wonder that He prayed, "If it be possible, let this cup pass from me"? Is Christ to be blamed for these shrinkings of nature? My dear friends, if it had been a pleasure to Him and He had had no shrinkings, where would have been His holy courage? If it had not been a horrible and dreadful thing to Him, where would have been His submission, where would have been the virtue that made atonement of it? If it had been a thing that He could not, or must not, shrink from, where would have been the pain, the wormwood, and the gall of it? The cup must be, in the nature of things, something from which He that bears it must shrink, or else it could not have been sufficient for the redemption of His people and the vindication of the broken law of God. It was necessary, then, that Christ should, by such a prayer as this, prove that He had overcome all the shrinkings of His nature.

"Not as I will," is also an evidence of *Christ's complete submission to the will of His Father.* "He is brought as a lamb to the slaughter, and as a sheep before her shearers is dumb, so he openeth not his mouth" (Isa. 57:3). There is no resistance, no struggling, He gives Himself up completely. "There," He seems to say to the Lord, "do what You will with Me. I yield Myself absolutely to Your will." There was on Christ's part no reserve, no wish even to make any reserve. I go further and say that Jesus willed as God willed, and even prayed that the will of God, from which His human nature at first shrank, might be fulfilled. "Nevertheless not as I will, but as thou wilt."

O brothers and sisters—for you both need this grace—pray God to help you to learn how to copy your Lord in this submission! Have you submitted to the Lord's will? Are you submitting now? Are not some of you like bullocks unaccustomed to the yoke? There is a text, you know, in Psalm 131, "My soul is even as a weaned child" (v. 2). I have sometimes thought that, for some of the Lord's children, the passage would have to be read, "My soul is even as a weaning child," and there are many of God's people who are very long in the weaning. You cannot get satisfaction and quiet and contentment can you? Can you give yourself up entirely to God that He may do whatever He likes with you? Have you some fear of a tumor or a cancer? Is there before you the prospect of a painful and dangerous operation? Is business going badly with you so that you will probably lose everything? Is a dear child sickening? Is the mother likely to be taken away? Will you have to lose your position and reputation if you are faithful to the Lord? Will you be exposed to cruel slanders? Will you probably be cast out of your situation if you do what is right? Come now, whatever you dread or expect, can you give yourself up wholly to God and say, "It is the LORD: let Him do what seemeth him good"? Your Lord and Master did so, He said, "Not as I will." Oh, that He might teach you this divine art of absolute resignation to the purpose and ordinance of God until you also should be able to say, "Not as I will"! Thus you will sing—

> I bow me to thy will, O God,
> And all thy ways adore;
> And every day I live I'll seek
> To please thee more and more.

Combine the Two Prayers

First, let me say, *Number One will help you very much to Number Two.* If you learn to pray with Christ, with the holy boldness that almost says, "Father, I will," you are the man who will know how to say, "Not as I will." Is it not strange that it should be so? It looks like a contradiction, but I am sure that it is not so. The man who can have his will with God is the very man who does not want his own way with God. He who

may have what he likes is the man who wishes to have what God likes.
You remember the good old woman who lay near to death, and one said
to her, "Do you not expect soon to die?" She answered, "I do not know
whether I shall live or die. What is more, I have no concern which way
it is." Then the friend asked, "But if you had your choice whether you
should live or die, which would you choose?" She replied, "I would
rather that the Lord's will should be done." "But suppose the Lord's
will were to leave it entirely to you to choose whichever you liked?"
"Then," she said, "I would kneel down and pray the Lord to choose for
me." And I do think that is the best way to live, not to have any choice
at all, but to ask the Lord to choose for you. You can always have your
way, you know, when your way is God's way. The sure way to carry out
self-will is when self-will is nothing else but God's will. Oh, that the
Lord would teach us this mighty power with Him in prayer! It will not
be given without much close fellowship with Him. Then, when we
know that we can have what we will of Him, we shall be in the right
state to say, "Not as I will."

The next remark that I would make is, that *Number Two is needful
for Number One.* That is to say, until you can say, "Not as I will," you
never will be able to say, "Father, I will." I believe that one reason why
people cannot prevail in prayer is because they will not yield to God,
they cannot expect God to yield to them. God does this and that with
you, and you quarrel with Him. Then you go upstairs and begin to pray.
Go down on your knees and make your peace with Him first. For if you
must not come to the altar until you have become reconciled to your
brother, how can you come to the throne of grace until you have given
up your quarrel with God? But some people are never at peace with
God. I have heard of a good friend who lost a child, and he was wearing mourning several years afterward. He was always fretting about the
dear child, until a Quakeress said to him, "What! have you not forgiven
God yet?" There are some people who have not yet forgiven God for
taking their loved ones. They ought always to have blessed Him for He
never takes away any but those whom He lent to us. We should bless
His name as much for taking them again as for lending them to us. Dear
friends, you must submit to the will of God or else you cannot have
power with Him in prayer. "Well," say you, "you will not let me have
my own way at all." Certainly, I will not let you have your own way.
But when you just say, "There, Lord, I have no quarrel with You now.
Do what You will with me." Then He will say, "Rise, my child, ask
what you will, and I will give it to you. 'Open thy mouth wide, and I
will fill it'" (Ps. 81:10).

Notice, also, dear friends, that *Jesus will help us to have Number
One and Number Two.* He gives Himself over to us to teach us the

power of prevailing prayer, but He also gives Himself over to teach us
the art of blessed submission in prayer. It is His will that these two
should not be separated. "Father, I will," is Christ's word on our behalf;
"Not as I will," is equally Christ's word on our behalf. When you cannot pray either of these prayers as you would, fall back upon Christ's
prayer and claim it as your own.

Lastly, I think that *true sonship will embody both Number One and
Number Two.* It is the true child of God, who knows that he is his
Father's child, who says, "Father, I will." He is often very bold where
another would be presumptuous. Oh, I have heard full often of somebody's prayers—I will not say who the somebody is—he seemed so familiar with God in his prayer. Oh, yes; I know! You love those very
stately prayers in which the bounds are set about the mount and no man
may dare to come near. You make the throne of grace to be like Sinai
was of old, of which the Lord said, "Whosoever toucheth the mount
shall be surely put to death: there shall not an hand touch it, but he shall
surely be stoned, or shot through; whether it be beast or man, it shall
not live" (Ex. 19:12–13). "Oh, but," you say, "so-and-so is so familiar
at the mercy seat!" Yes, I know. And you think that is a pity, do you
not? Perhaps you are acquainted with a judge. Look at him on the
bench wearing his wig and robe of office, but you will not dare to speak
to him there unless you address him as "My lord" and behave very re-
spectfully to him. By-and-by he goes home, and he has a little boy
there, Master Johnny. Why, the child has seized hold of his father's
whiskers, there he is up on his father's back! "Why, Johnny, you are
disrespectful!" "Oh, but he is my father!" says the boy. His father says,
"Yes, Johnny, that I am. I do not want you to say, 'My lord,' and talk to
me as they do in the court." So, there are certain liberties which God's
children may take with Him which He counts no liberties at all, but He
loves so to be treated by them. He will let each one of them say,
"Father, I will," because they are His children.

Then, mark you, you are not God's child unless you can also say,
"Father, not as I will." The true child bends before his father's will.
"Yes," says he, "I would like so-and-so." His father forbids it. "Then I
do not want it, and I will not touch it." Or he says, "I do not like to take
that medicine, but my father says I am to take it," and he takes the cup
and drinks the whole of its contents. The true child says, "Not as I
will," although, after his measure, he also says, "Father, I will."

I have only been talking to you who are the Lord's people. I hope
you have learned something from this subject. I know you have if the
Lord has taught you to pray after the fashion of these two prayers, as
you humbly yet believingly may, copying your Lord.

But oh, what shall I say to those of you who are not the Lord's people? If you do not know how to pray at all, may the Lord teach you! If you do not yet know your needs, may the Lord instruct you! But let me tell you that if ever there shall come a time when you feel your need of a Savior, the Lord Jesus will be willing to receive you. If ever you should yearn after Him, be sure that He is also yearning after you. Even now—

> Kindled his relentings are,

and if you will but breathe the penitent's prayer, "God be merciful to me, a sinner" (Luke 18:13), and turn your eye Christ-ward, and cross-ward, there is salvation for you even now. God grant that you may have it, for Jesus' sake! Amen.

12

"Love and I"—A Mystery

I have declared unto them thy name, and will declare it: that the love wherewith thou hast loved me may be in them, and I in them (John 17:26).

For several Sunday mornings my mind has been directed into subjects which I might fitly call the deep things of God. I think I have never felt my own incompetence more fully than in trying to handle such subjects. It is a soil into which one may dig and dig as deep as ever you will, and still never exhaust the golden nuggets which lie within it. I am, however, comforted by this fact, that these subjects are so fruitful that even we who can only scratch the surface of them shall yet get a harvest from them. I read once of the plains of India that they were so fertile that you had only to tickle them with a hoe and they laughed with plenty. Surely such a text as this may be described as equally fruitful, even under our feeble husbandry. Pearls lie on the surface here as well as in the depth. We have only to search its surface and stir the soil a little, and we shall be astonished at the plenitude of spiritual wealth which lies before us. Oh, that the Spirit of God may help us to enjoy the blessed truths which are herein set forth! Here is the priceless treasure, but it lies hid until He reveals it to us.

You see, this text is taken out of our Lord's last prayer with His disciples. He did as good as say, "I am about to leave you; I am about to die for you. For awhile you will not see me, but now, before we separate, let us pray." It is one of those impulses that you have felt yourselves. When you have been about to part from those you love, to leave them perhaps in danger and difficulty, you have felt you could do no less than say, "Let us draw nigh unto God." Your heart found no way of expressing itself at all so fitting, so congenial, so satisfactory as to

This sermon was taken from *The Metropolitan Tabernacle Pulpit* and was preached on Sunday morning, July 2, 1882.

draw near to the great Father and spread the case before Him. Now, a prayer from such a one as Jesus, our Lord and Master; a prayer in such a company, with the eleven whom He had chosen and who had consorted with Him from the beginning; a prayer under such circumstances, when He was just on the brink of the brook of Cedron, and there lay down His life—such a prayer as this, so living, earnest, loving, and divine, deserves the most studious meditations of all believers. I invite you to bring hither your best thoughts and skill for the navigation of this sea. It is not a creek or bay, but the main ocean itself. We cannot hope to fathom its depths. This is true of any sentence of this matchless prayer. But for me the work of exposition becomes unusually heavy because my text is the close and climax of this marvelous supplication. It is the central mystery of all. In the lowest depth there is still a lower deep, and this verse is one of those deeps which still exceed the rest. Oh, how much we want the Spirit of God. Pray for His bedewing: pray that His balmy influences may descend upon us richly now.

You will observe that the last word of our Lord's prayer is concerning *love*. This is the last petition which He offers, "That the love wherewith thou hast loved me may be in them, and I in them." He reaches no greater height than this, namely, that His people be filled with the Father's love. How could He rise higher? For this is to be filled with all the fullness of God, since God is love, and He that loves dwells in God and God in Him. What importance ought you and I to attach to the grace of love! How highly we should esteem that which Jesus makes the crown jewel of all. If we have faith, let us not be satisfied unless our faith works by love and purifies the soul. Let us not be content indeed until the love of Christ is shed abroad in our hearts by the Holy Spirit which is given to us. Well did the poet say,

> Only love to us be given,
> Lord, we ask no other heaven.

For indeed there is no other heaven above than to reach to the fullness of perfect love. This is where the prayer of the Son of David ends, in praying "that the love wherewith thou hast loved me may be in them." What a subject! The highest that even our Lord Jesus reached in His noblest prayer. Again with groanings my heart cries, Holy Spirit, help.

I shall this morning try to speak first upon *the food of love*, or what love lives upon. Secondly, upon *the love itself, what kind of love it is*. Then, thirdly, upon *the companion of love*. "That the love wherewith thou hast loved me may be in them, and I in them."

The Food of Love to God

What is it? *It is knowledge.* "I have declared unto them thy name, and will declare it." We cannot love a God whom we do not know. A measure of knowledge is needful to affection. However lovely God may be, a man blind of soul cannot perceive Him and, therefore, is not touched by His loveliness. Only when the eyes are opened to behold the loveliness of God will the heart go out toward God who is so desirable an object for the affections. Friends, we must know in order to believe; we must know in order to hope, we must especially know in order to love. Hence the great desirableness that you should know the Lord and His great love which passes knowledge. You cannot reciprocate love that you have never known, even as a man cannot derive strength from food that he has not eaten. Until first of all the love of God has come into your heart and you have been made a partaker of it, you cannot rejoice in it or return it. Therefore our Lord took care to feed His disciples' hearts upon the Father's name. He labored to make the Father known to them. This is one of His great efforts with them. He is grieved when He sees their ignorance and has to say to one of them, "Have I been so long time with you, and yet hast thou not known me, Philip? He that hath seen me hath seen the Father; and how sayest thou then, Show us the Father?" (John 14:9). Study much, then, the Word of God. Be diligent in turning the pages of Scripture and in hearing God's true ministers that the flame of love within your hearts may be revived by the fuel of holy knowledge which you place upon it. Pile on the logs of sandalwood, and let the perfumed fires burn before the Lord. Heap on the handfuls of frankincense and sweet odors of sacred knowledge that on the altar of your heart there may always be burning the sacred flame of love to God in Christ Jesus.

The knowledge here spoken of is *a knowledge that Jesus gave them.* "I have known thee, and these have known that thou hast sent me. And I have declared unto them thy name, and will declare it" (17:25–26). O beloved, it is not knowledge that you and I pick up as a matter of book learning that will ever bring out our love to the Father. It is knowledge given us by Christ through His Spirit. It is not knowledge communicated by the preacher alone that will bless you. However much he may be taught of God himself, he cannot preach to the heart unless the blessed Spirit of God comes and takes of the things that are spoken and reveals them and makes them manifest to each individual heart, so that in consequence it knows the Lord. Jesus said, "O righteous Father, the world hath not known thee" (v. 25). You and I would have been in the same condition—strangers to God, without God and without hope in the world—if the Spirit of God had not taken of divine things and applied them to our souls so that we are made to know them. Every living word of knowledge is the work of the living God. If you only know what you have found out for yourself or picked up by your own industry apart from Jesus, you know nothing aright. It must be by the direct and distinct teaching of God the Holy Spirit that you must learn to profit. Jesus Christ alone can reveal the Father. He Himself said, "No man cometh unto the Father but by me" (14:6). He that knows not Christ knows not the Father. But when Jesus Christ reveals Him, ah! then we do know Him after a special, personal, peculiar, inward knowledge. This knowledge brings with it a life and a love with which the soul is not puffed up, but built up. By such knowledge we grow up into Him in all things who is our head, being taught of the Son of God.

This knowledge, dear friends, *comes to us gradually.* The text indicates this. "I have declared unto them thy name, and will declare it." As if, though they knew the Father, there was far more to know and the Lord Jesus was resolved to teach them more. Are you growing in knowledge, my brothers and sisters? My labor is lost if you are not growing in grace and in the knowledge of our Lord and Savior Jesus Christ. I hope you know much more of God than you did twenty years ago when first you came to Him. That little knowledge which you received by grace when you found "life in a look at the Crucified One" has saved you. But in these after years you have added to your faith knowledge, and to your knowledge experience. You have gone on to know more deeply what you knew before, and to know the details of what you seemed to know in the gross and the lump at first. You have come to look *into* things as well as *upon* things—a look at Christ saves. But oh, it is the look *into* Christ that wins the heart's love and holds it fast and binds us to Him as with fetters of gold. We ought every day to be adding something to this inestimably precious store that as we are known of God so we may know God and become thereby transformed from glory to glory through His Spirit.

Are you not thankful for this blessed word of the Lord Jesus: "I will declare it"; "I will make it known"? He did do so at His resurrection when He taught His people things they knew not before. But He did so much more after He had ascended upon high when the Spirit of God was given. "He shall teach you all things, and bring all things to your remembrance, whatsoever I have said unto you" (14:26). And now today in the hearts of His people He is daily teaching us something that we do not know. All our experience tends that way. When the Spirit of God blesses an affliction to us, it is one of the Savior's illuminated books out of which we learn something more of the Father's name, and consequently come to love Him better. That is the thing Christ aims at.

He would so make known the Father that the love wherewith the Father has loved Him may be in us, and that He Himself may be in us.

This knowledge distinguishes us from the world. It is the mark by which the elect are made manifest. In the sixth verse of chapter seventeen our Lord says: "I have manifested thy name unto the men which thou gavest me out of the world: thine they were, and thou gavest them me; and they have kept thy word." The world does not know the Father and cannot know Him, for it abides in the darkness and death of sin. Judge yourselves therefore by this sure test, and let the love which grows out of gracious knowledge be a token for good to you.

Now let me try to show you what the Savior meant when He said, "I have declared unto them thy name, and will declare it." This knowledge which breeds love is *knowledge of the name of God.* What does He mean by "Thy name." Now, I do not think I should preach an unprofitable sermon if I were to stop with the connection and say that the "name" here meant is specially the name used in the twenty-fifth verse: "O righteous Father, the world hath not known thee." This is the name which we most need to know—"righteous Father." Observe the singular combination here. Righteous, and yet a Father. *"Righteous"*—to us poor sinners that is a word of terror when we first hear it. "Father"—oh, how sweet. That is a word of good cheer even to us prodigals. But we are afraid to lay hold upon it for our sins arise and our consciences protest that God must be righteous and punish sin.

Our joy begins when we see the two united: "righteous Father"—a Father full of love, and nothing but love, to His people; yet righteous as a Judge, as righteous as if He were no Father. Dealing out His righteousness with stern severity as the Judge of all the earth must do, and yet a Father at the same time. I do protest that I never did love God at all, nor could I embrace Him in my affections until I understood how He could be just and yet the justifier of Him that believes in Jesus: how, in a word, He could be the "righteous Father." That satisfied my conscience and my heart at the same time, for my conscience said, It is well. God has not put away sin without a sacrifice and has not winked at sin nor waived His justice in order to indulge His mercy, but He remains just as He ever was—the same thrice holy God who will by no means spare the guilty. He has laid the punishment of our sins upon Christ. He has made Him to be sin for us who knew no sin that we might be made the righteousness of God in Him. And all this He has done that He might act to us as a Father, and save His own children from the result of their transgression.

He has given His only begotten Son to die in our stead that many sons might be brought to glory through Him. It is at the cross we understand this riddle. Here we see the righteous Father. But the world will not learn it, and a large part of the professing church, which is nothing better than the world wrongfully named with Christ's name, will not learn it. They do anything they can to get away from atonement. Love without righteousness is their idol. Substitution is a word that is hard for the world to spell. They cannot abide it. That Christ should suffer in the stead of the guilty and bear that we might never bear the Father's righteous wrath—this they cannot away with. Many pretend to keep the atonement, and yet they tear the bowels out of it. They profess to believe in the Gospel, but it is a gospel without the blood of the atonement. A bloodless gospel is a lifeless gospel, a dead gospel, and a damning gospel. Let those take heed who cannot see God as a righteous Father, for they are numbered among the world who know Him not. "These have known thee," says our Lord. These who have been taught by Christ, and these alone, come to find as much joy in the word "righteous" as in the word "Father."

Blending the two together they feel an intense love to the "righteous Father." Their hearts rejoice in a holy Gospel, a message of mercy consistent with justice, a covenant salvation ordered in all things and sure, because it does no violence to law and does not bind the hands of justice. Beloved, if this revelation of the atoning blood does not make your heart love Jesus and love the Father, it is because you are not in Him. But if you know this secret as to how righteousness and peace have kissed each other, you know the name that wins the affection of believers to God. My own heart is glad and rejoices every hour because I find rest in substitution, safety in the vindication of the law, and bliss in the glory of the divine character.

> Lo! in the grace that rescued man
> His brightest form of glory shines!
> Here, on the cross, 'tis fairest drawn
> In precious blood and crimson lines.
>
> Here I behold His inmost heart,
> Where grace and vengeance strangely join,
> Piercing his Son with sharpest smart,
> To make the purchased pleasure mine.
>
> Oh, the sweet wonders of that cross,
> Where God the Saviour loved and died!
> Her noblest life my spirit draws
> From his dear wounds and bleeding sides.

Still, I would take the word "name" *in a wider sense.* "I have declared unto them thy name," which signifies "thy character." The word "name" is used as a sort of summary of all the attributes of God. All these attributes are well adapted to win the love of all regenerate spirits. Just think for a minute. God is *holy*. To a holy mind there is nothing in the world, there is nothing in heaven more beautiful than holiness. We read of the beauties of holiness. To a soul that is purified, holiness is superlatively lovely. Now, beauty wins love. Consequently when Jesus Christ makes known His holy Father, and shows us in His life and in His death the holiness of the Ever-blessed, then our heart is won to the Father. "Oh," say you, "but holiness does not always win love." No, not the love of the defiled hearts that cannot appreciate it. But those who are pure in heart, and can see God, no sooner behold His holiness than they are enamored of it, and their souls at once delight in their Lord.

Moreover, we learn from our Lord Jesus that God is *good*. "There is none good but one, that is, God" (Matt 19:17; Mark 10:18). How inexpressibly good He is! There is no goodness but what comes from God. His name, "God," is but short for "good," and all the good things that we receive in this life and for the life to come are but enlargements of His blessed name. "Every good gift and every perfect gift is from above, and cometh down from the Father of lights" (James 1:17). Blessings enjoyed by us are streams that flow from the fountain head of God's infinite goodness to the sons of men. A man cannot help loving God when once he knows Him to be good, for all men love that which they apprehend to be good to them. A man says, "Gold is good; rest is good; fame is good"; and therefore he seeks after these things, and when he comes to know that God is good, oh, then his spirit follows hard after him. He cannot help but love that which he is persuaded is in the highest sense good. The soul that knows the name of the Lord rejoices at the very mention of Him.

To sinners like ourselves perhaps the next word may have more sweetness. God is *merciful*; He is ever ready to forgive. Note how the prophet says, "Who is a God like unto thee, . . . and passeth by the transgression?" (Mic. 7:18). He does not say, "Who is a *man* like unto thee?" for none among our race can for a moment be compared with Him. But even if the gods of the heathen were gods, none of them could be likened to the Lord for mercy. Now, when a man knows that He has offended, and yet the person offended readily and freely forgives, why, it wins his love. If he is a right-hearted man he cries, "I cannot again offend one who so generously casts all my offenses behind his back." The mercy of God is such a love-winning attribute that, as I told you the other Sunday, twenty-six times in a single psalm the ancient church sang, "His mercy endureth forever" (118). Free grace and pardoning love sensibly known in the would will win your hearts to God forever, so that you shall be His willing servants as long as you have any being.

But then there is a higher word still. God is *love,* and there is something about love that always wins love. When love puts on her own golden armor and bares her sword bright with her own unselfishness, she goes on conquering and to conquer. Let a man once apprehend that God is love, that this is God's very essence, and he must at once love God. I do not mean merely "apprehend" that God is love in the cold intellect. But when this heart begins to glow and burn with that divine revelation, then straightway the spirit is joined to the Lord, and rests with delight in the great Father of Spirits. Love knits and binds. Oh to feel more of its uniting power.

Thus have I shown you the manna that love feeds upon, the nectar that it drinks. Everything in God is lovely, and there is no trait in His character that is otherwise than lovely. All the lovelinesses that can be conceived are heaped up in God without the slightest admixture of adulteration. He is love altogether, wholly, and emphatically. Oh, surely our Lord and Master was wise when He led His people's love upon such meat as this.

Friends, we have as yet only been standing at the furnace mouth. Let us now enter into the devouring flame.

The Love Itself

Observe, first, *what this love is not.* "I have declared unto them thy name, and will declare it: that the love wherewith thou hast loved me may be *in* them." Do notice that the prayer is not that the Father's love may be set *upon* them or moved toward them. God does not love us because we know Him, for He loved us before we knew Him, even as Paul speaks of "His great love wherewith he loved us, even when we were dead in sins" (Eph. 2:4–5). Jesus has not come to set His Father's love upon the chosen. Oh, no; He did not even die with that object, for the Father's love was upon the chosen from everlasting. "The Father himself loveth you" (John 16:27) was always true. Christ did not die to make His Father loving, but because His Father is loving. The atoning blood is the outflow of the very heart of God toward us. So do not make any mistake. Our Lord speaks not of the divine love in itself, but in us. This is not the eternal love of God *toward* us of which we are now reading, but that love *in* us. We are inwardly to feel the love that proceeds from the Father, and so to have it *in* us. We are to have the love of God shed abroad in our hearts by the Holy Spirit that is given to us. It is to be recognized by us, felt in us, made the subject of inward joy. This it is that our Lord wishes to produce, that the love of God may be in us, dwelling in our hearts, a welcome guest, the sovereign of our souls.

And this love is *of a very peculiar sort.* Do let me read the verse again: "That the love wherewith thou hast loved me may be in them." It is God's own love in us. The love of the Father toward Jesus springs up like a crystal fountain, and then the sparkling drops fall and overflow, as you have seen the fountains do. We are the cups into which this overflowing love of God toward Christ Jesus flows, and flows until we too are full. The inward love so much desired for us by our Lord is no emotion of nature, no attachment proceeding from the unregenerate will. But it is the Father's love transplanted into the soil of these poor hearts and becoming our love to Jesus, as we shall have to show in the next point. But is not this a wonderful thing—that God's own love to Jesus should dwell in our hearts? And yet it is so. The love wherewith we love Christ, mark you, is God's love to Christ: "That the love wherewith thou hast loved me may be in them." All true love, such as the Father delights in and accepts at our hands, is nothing but His own love that has come streaming down from His own heart into our renewed minds.

But what can this mean? I must ask you to observe that it includes within itself four precious things.

First, the text means that *our Lord Jesus Christ desires us to have a distinct recognition of the Father's love to Him.* He wants the love wherewith the Father loves Him to be felt in us, so that we may say, "Yes, I know the Father loved Him, for I, who am such a poor, unworthy, and foolish creature, yet love Him. Oh, how His Father must love Him." I love him! Aye, by His grace, it were a blessed thing to die for Him. But if I love Him, oh, how must His Father love Him who can see all His beauty, and can appreciate every distinct piece of loveliness that is in Him! God never loved anything as He loves Christ, except His people, and they have had to be lifted up to that position by the love which the Father has to His Son. For, first and foremost, the Father and the Son are one—they are one in essence. The Savior has been with the Father from the beginning, and His delight has been with Him, even as the Father testified, "This is my beloved Son, in whom I am well pleased" (Matt. 3:17; 17:5; 2 Peter 1:17). Oh, do try to feel, if you can, the love of the Father to His Son, or else you will not love the Father as you should for the amazing sacrifice which He made in giving Jesus to us. Think what it cost Him to tear His well-Beloved from His bosom and send Him down below to be "despised and rejected" (Isa. 53:3). Think what it cost Him to nail Him up to yonder cross, and then forsake Him and hide His face from Him because He had laid all our sins upon Him. Oh, the love He must have had to us thus to have made His best Beloved to become a curse for us, as it is written, "Cursed is every one that hangeth on a tree" (Gal. 3:13). I want you to get this right into your souls, dear friends. Do not hold it as a dry doctrine, but let it touch your heart. Let it flow into your heart like a boiling stream until your whole soul becomes like Icelandic geysers, which boil and bubble up and send their steam aloft into the clouds. Oh, to have the soul filled with the love of the Father toward Him who is altogether lovely.

Now, go a step further and deeper. Our text bears a further reading. Remember that *you are to have in your heart a sense of the Father's love to you,* and to recollect that it is precisely the same love wherewith He loves His Son. "That the love wherewith thou hast loved me may be in them." Oh, wonder of wonders, I feel more inclined to sit down and meditate upon it than to stand up and talk about it! The love wherewith He loved His Son—such is His love to all His chosen ones. Can you believe it, that you should be the object of God's delight, even as Christ is, because you are in Christ. That you should be the object of the Father's love as truly as Christ is, because He sees you to be part and parcel of the mystical body of His well-beloved Son? Do not tell me that God the Father does not love you as well as He does Christ. The point can be settled by the grandest matter of fact that ever was. When there was a choice between Christ and His people which should die of the two, the Father freely delivered up His own Son that we might live through Him. Oh, what a meeting there must have been of the seas of love that day, when God's great love to us came rolling in like a glorious springtide, and His love to His Son came rolling in at the same time. If they had met and come into collision, we cannot imagine the result but when they both took to riding together in one mighty torrent, what a stream of love was there! The Lord Jesus sank that we might swim; He sank that we might rise. Now we are borne onward forever by the mighty sweep of infinite love into an everlasting blessedness which tongues and lips can never fully set forth. Oh, be ravished with this. Be carried away with it; be in ecstasy at love so amazing, so divine. The Father loves you even as He loves His Son. After the same manner and sort He loves all His redeemed.

But now this goes to a third meaning, and that is that *we are to give back a reflection of this love and to love Jesus as the Father loves Him.* A dear old friend speaking to me the other day in a rapturous tone said, "I love Jesus as the Father loves Him." This is true; not equally, but like. Is not this a blessed thought? I said, "O friend, that is a strong thing to say!" "Ah," said he, "but not stronger than Jesus would have it when He prays that 'the love wherewith thou hast loved me may be in them, and I in them.'" His people love Christ as the Father loves Him—in the same way, though from want of capacity they cannot reach to the same immeasurable force of love. Oh, to throw back on Christ His Father's love. The Father is the sun and we are the moon, but the moonlight is the same light as the sunlight. We can see a difference because reflection robs the light of much of its heat and its brilliance, but it is the same light. The moon has not a ray of light but what came from the sun, and we have not a live coal of love to Christ but what came from the Father. We are as the moon, shining by reflected light, but Jesus loves the moonlight of our love and rejoices in it. Let us give Him all of it. Let us try to be as the full moon always and not dwindle down to a mere ring of love or a crescent of affection. Let us render no half-moon love. Let us not be half dark and cold, but let us shine on Christ with all the light we can possibly reflect of His Father's love saying in our very soul,

> My Jesus, I love thee, I know thou art mine;
> For thee all the follies of sin I resign.

And then, fourthly, *this love of the Father in us is to go beaming forth from us to all around.* When we get the love wherewith the Father loves the Son into our hearts, then it is to go out toward all the chosen seed. He that loves Him that begat loves also them that are begotten of Him. Aye, and your love is to go forth to all the sons of men, seeking their good for God's glory, that they may be brought in to know the same Savior in whom we rejoice. Oh, if the love of the Father to Christ once enters into a man's soul it will change him. It will sway him with the noblest passion. It will make him a zealot for Christ. It will cast out His selfishness. It will change Him into the image of Christ and fit him to dwell in heaven where love is perfected.

So I conclude this second head by saying that this indwelling of the Father's love in us has the most blessed results. It has an *expulsive* result. As soon as ever it gets into the heart it says to all love of sin, "Get you hence; there remains no room for you here." When the light enters in, the darkness receives immediate notice of ejectment. The night is gone as soon as the dawn appears. It has also a *repulsive* power by which it repels the assaults of sin. As though a man did snatch the sun out of the heaven and make a round shield with it, and hold it in the very face of the prince of darkness, and blind him with the light, so does the love of God the Father repel the enemy. It girds the soul with the armor of light. It repels the Devil, the love of the world, the love of sin, and all outward temptations.

And then what an *impulsive* power it has. Get the love of Christ into you, and it is as when an engine receives fire and steam, and so obtains the force that drives it. Then have you strengthening, then have you motive power, then are you urged on to this and that heroic deed which, apart from this sublime love, you never would have thought. For Christ you can live, for Christ you can suffer, for Christ you can die, when once the Father's love to Him has taken full possession of your spirit. And, oh, how elevating it is. How it lifts a man up above self and sin. How it makes him seek the things that are above! How purifying it is; how happy it makes the subject of its influence.

If you are unhappy you want more of the love of God. "Oh," say you, "I want a larger income." Nonsense. A man is not made happy by money. You will do very well in poverty if you have enough of the love of God. Oh, but if your soul be filled with the love of God your spirit will be ready to dance at the very sound of His name. You murmur and repine at providence because the fire of your love is burning low. Come, get the ashes together. Pray the Spirit of God to blow upon them. Beg Him to bring fresh fuel of holy knowledge until your soul becomes like Nebuchadnezzar's furnace, heated seven times hotter. This is the kind of love we should have toward Christ. No blessing can excel it. Oh, Savior, let your prayer be fulfilled in me and in all your dear people this morning, and may the love wherewith the Father has loved you be in us.

The Companion of Love

"I in them." Look at the text a minute and just catch those two words. Here is "love" and "I"—love and Christ come together. Oh, blessed guests! "Love and I," says Christ; as if He felt He never had a companion that suited Him better. "Love" and "I"—Jesus is ever at home where love is reigning. When love lives in His people's hearts, Jesus lives there too. Does Jesus, then, live in the hearts of His people? Yes; wherever there is the love of the Father shed abroad in them He must be there. We have His own word for it, and we are sure that Jesus knows where He is.

We are sure that He is where love is. First, where there is love there is *life,* and where there is life there is Christ, for He Himself says, "I am the . . . life" (John 6:35; 11:25; 14:6). There is no true life in the believer's soul that is divided from Christ. We are sure of that; so that where there is love there is life, and where there is life there is Christ. Again, where there is the love of God in the heart there is *the Holy Spirit.* But wherever the Holy Spirit is, there is Christ, for the Holy Spirit is Christ's representative. It is in that sense that He tells us, "Lo, I am with you alway" (Matt. 28:20), namely, because the Spirit has come to be with us always. So where there is love there is the Spirit of God, and where there is the Spirit of God there is Christ. So it is always "love and I."

Furthermore, where there is love there is *faith,* for faith works by love, and there never was true love to Christ apart from faith. But where there is faith there is always Christ, for if there is faith in Him He has been received into the soul. Jesus is ever near to that faith which has Himself for its foundation and resting place. Where there is love there is faith, where there is faith there is Christ, and so it is "love and I."

Aye, but where there is the Father's love toward Christ in the heart

God Himself is there. I am sure of that, for God is love. So if there is love within us there must be God, and where God is there Christ is, for He says, "I and my Father are one" (John 10:30). So you see where there is love there must be Jesus Christ, for these reasons and for many others beside.

"I in them." Yes, if I were commanded to preach for seven years from these three words only, I should never exhaust the text, I am quite certain. I might exhaust you by my dullness, and exhaust myself by labor to tell out the sacred secret, but I would never exhaust the text. "I in them." It is the most blessed word I know. You, beloved, need not go abroad to find the Lord Jesus Christ. Where does He live? He lives within you. "I in them." As soon as ever you pray you are sure He hears you because He is within you. He is not knocking at your door. He has entered into you, and there He dwells and will go no more out forever.

What a blessed sense of power this gives to us. "I in them." Then it is no more "I" in weakness, but, since Jesus dwells in me, "I can do all things through Christ which strengtheneth me" (Phil. 4:13). "I in them." It is the glory of the believer that Christ dwells in him. "Unto you therefore which believe he is precious" (1 Peter 2:7).

Hence we gather the security of the believer. If Christ be in me, and I am overcome, Christ is conquered too, for He is in me. "I in them." I cannot comprehend the doctrine of believers falling from grace. If Christ has once entered into them, will He not abide with them? Paul says, "I am persuaded, that neither death, nor life, nor angels, nor principalities, nor powers, nor things present, nor things to come, nor height, nor depth, nor any other creature, shall be able to separate us from the love of God which is in Christ Jesus our Lord" (Rom. 8:38–39). To that persuasion I set my hand and seal. Well, then, if Christ is in us, whatever happens to us will happen to Him. We shall be losers if we do not get to heaven. But so will He be, for He is in us and so is a partaker of our condition. If it is an indissoluble union—and so He declares it is, "I in them"—then His destiny and ours are linked together. If He wins the victory, we conquer in Him. If He sits at the right hand of God, we shall sit at the right hand of God with Him, for He is in us.

I know not what more to say, not because I have nothing more, but because I do not know which to bring forward out of a thousand precious things. But I leave the subject with you. Go home and live in the power of this blessed text. Go home and be as happy as you can be to live. If you get a little happier that will not hurt you, for then you will be in heaven. Keep up unbroken joy in the Lord. It is not "I in them" for Sundays and away on Mondays, nor "I in them" when they sit in the Tabernacle and out of them when they reach home. No; "I in them," and that forever and forever. Go and rejoice. Show this blind world that you have a happiness which as much outshines theirs as the sun outshines the sparks that fly from the chimney and expire. Go forth with joy and be led forth with peace. Let the mountains and the hills break forth before you into singing.

> All that remains for me
> Is but to love and sing,
> And wait until the angels come,
> To bear me to the King.

"Oh, but I have my troubles." I know you have your troubles, but they are not worthy to be compared with the glory that shall be revealed in you, nor even with your present glory. I feel as if I could not think about troubles, nor sins, nor anything else when I once behold the love of God to me. When I feel my love to Christ, which is but God's love to Christ, burning within my soul, then I glory in tribulation, for the power of God shall be through these afflictions made manifest in me. "I in them." God bless you with the knowledge of this mystery, for Jesus' sake. Amen.

13

Christian Resignation

Not as I will, but as thou wilt (Matthew 26:39).

The apostle Paul, writing concerning our Lord Jesus Christ, says, "Though he were a Son, yet learned he obedience by the things which he suffered" (Heb. 5:8). He who, as God, knew all things had to learn obedience in the time of His humiliation. He, who is in Himself Wisdom Incarnate, did Himself condescend to enter the school of suffering, there to learn that important lesson of the Christian life, obedience to the will of God. Here, in Gethsemane's garden, you can see the Divine Scholar going forth to practice His lesson. He had been all His lifetime learning it, and now He has to learn it for the last time in His agony and bloody sweat and in His terrible death upon the cross. Now is He to discover the utmost depths of suffering and to attain to the height of the knowledge of obedience. See how well He has learned His lesson. Note how complete and ripe a scholar He is. He has attained to the very highest class in that school. And, in the immediate prospect of death, can say to His Father, "Not as I will, but as thou wilt."

The object of this discourse is to commend to you the blessed example of our Lord Jesus Christ. As God the Holy Spirit shall help me to urge you to be made like to your glorious Head, and yourselves to learn, by all the daily providences with which God is pleased to surround you, this lesson of resignation to the will of God and of making an entire surrender to Him.

I have been struck, lately, in reading works by some writers who belong to the Romish Church with the marvelous love which they have toward the Lord Jesus Christ. I did think, at one time, that it could not be possible for any to be saved in that church. But, often, after I have risen from reading the books of those holy men and have felt myself to be

---

This sermon was taken from *The Metropolitan Tabernacle Pulpit* and was preached on a Thursday evening early in the year 1859.

quite a dwarf by their side, I have said, "Yes, despite their errors, these men must have been taught of the Holy Spirit. Notwithstanding all the evils of which they have drunk so deeply, I am quite certain that they must have had fellowship with Jesus, or else they could not have written as they did." Such writers are few and far between. But, still, there is a remnant according to the election of grace even in the midst of that apostate church. Looking at a book by one of them the other day, I met with this remarkable expression, "Shall that body, which has a thorn-crowned Head, have delicate, pain-fearing members? God forbid!" That remark went straight to my heart at once. I thought how often the children of God shun pain, reproach, and rebuke, and think it to be a strange thing when some fiery trial happens to them. If they would but recollect that their Head had to sweat as it were great drops of blood falling down to the ground, and that their Head was crowned with thorns, it would not seem strange to them that the members of His mystical body also have to suffer. If Christ had been some delicate person, if our glorious Head had been reposing upon the soft pillow of ease, then might we, who are the members of His church, have expected to go through this world with joy and comfort. But if He must be bathed in His own blood, if the thorns must pierce His temples, if His lips must be parched, and if His mouth must be dried up like a furnace, shall we escape suffering and agony? Is Christ to have a head of brass and bands of gold? Is His head to be as if it glowed in the furnace and are not we to glow in the furnace, too? Must He pass through seas of suffering, and shall we—

> Be carried to the skies,
> On flowery beds of ease?

Ah, no! we must be conformed to our Lord in His humiliation if we would be made like Him also in His glory.

So, brethren and sisters, I have to discourse to you upon this lesson, which some of us have begun to learn, but of which as yet we know so little—this lesson of saying, "Not as I will, but as thou wilt." First, let me *explain the meaning of this prayer.* Then, let me *urge you, by certain reasons, to make this your constant cry.* Next, let me *show what will be the happy effect of its being the paramount desire of your spirits.* We will then conclude with a practical inquiry—*what can bring us to this blessed condition?*

What Is the Meaning of This Prayer

I shall not address myself to those Christians who are but as dwarfs, who know little about the things of the kingdom. I will speak rather to those who do business in the deep waters of communion, who know what it is to pillow their heads upon the bosom of Jesus, to walk with

God as Enoch did, and to talk with him as Abraham did. My dear friends, only such as you can understand this prayer in all its length and breadth. Your friend, who as yet scarcely knows the meaning of the word communion, may pray thus in some feeble measure. Yet it is not to be expected that he should discern all the spiritual teaching that there is in these words of our Lord. But to you who are Christ-taught, you who have become ripe scholars in the school of Christ, to you I may speak as to wise men—judge what I say.

If you and I mean this prayer and do not use it as a mere form of words, but mean it in all its fullness, we must be prepared for this kind of experience. Sometimes, when we are in the midst of the most active service, when we are diligently serving God both with our hands and our heart, and when success is crowning all our labors, the Lord will lay us aside, take us right away from the vineyard, and thrust us into the furnace. Just at the very time when the church seems to need us most, when the world's necessities are most of all appealing to us, and when our hearts are full of love toward Christ and toward our fellow-creatures, it will often happen that, just then, God will strike us down with sickness or remove us from our sphere of activity. But if we really mean this prayer, we must be prepared to say, "Not as I will, but as thou wilt."

This is not easy, for does not the Holy Spirit Himself teach us to long after active service for our Savior? Does He not, when He gives us love toward our fellow men, constrain us, as it were, to make their salvation our meat and our drink? When He is actively at work within our hearts, do we not feel as if we could not live without solving God? Do we not then feel that to labor for the Lord is our highest rest, and that toil for Jesus is our sweetest pleasure? Does it not then seem most trying to our ardent spirit to be compelled to drink the cup of sickness and to be incapable of doing anything actively for God? The preacher is seeing men converted and his ministry successful, but, on a sudden, he is compelled to cease from preaching. Or the Sunday school teacher has, by the grace of God, been the means of bringing his class into an interesting and hopeful condition. Yet, just when the class needs his presence most, he is smitten down so that he cannot go on with his work. Ah! then it is that the spirit finds it hard to say, "Not as I will, but as thou wilt." But if we adopt this prayer, this is what it means: that we should be prepared to suffer instead of to serve, and should be as willing to be in the trenches as to scale the walls, and as willing to be laid aside in the King's hospital as to be fighting in the midst of the rank and file of the King's army. This is hard to flesh and blood, but we must do it if we present this petition.

If we really mean this prayer, there will be a second trial for us. Sometimes, *God will demand of us that we labor in unpropitious fields.*

He will set His children to plow the rock and to cast their bread upon
the waters. He will send His Ezekiel to prophesy in a valley full of dry
bones, and His Jonah to carry His message to Nineveh. He will give His
servants strange work to do—work that seems as if it never could be
successful, or bring honor either to God or to themselves. I doubt not
that there are some ministers who toil and labor with all their might, yet
who see but little fruit. Far away in the dark places of heathendom,
there are men who have been toiling for years with scarcely a convert to
cheer them. Here, too, in England, there are men who are preaching, in
all sincerity and faithfulness, the Word of the Lord, yet they do not see
souls converted. They know that they are to God a sweet savor of
Christ, both in them that perish and in them that are saved. Our hearts
are, I trust, so full of the Spirit prompting us to cry like Rachel, "Give
me children, or else I die" (Gen. 30:1), that we cannot rest content
without fleeing the success of our labors. Yet the Master, in effect, says
to us, "No, I tell you to continue to toil for me, though I give you no
fruit for your labor. You are to keep on plowing this rock, simply because I tell you to do it." Ah! then, friends, it is hard to say, "Not my
will, but thine, be done" (Luke 22:42). But we must say it. We must feel
that we are ready to forego even the joy of harvest and the glory of success, if God wills it.

At other times, God will remove His people from positions of honorable service to other offices that are far inferior in the minds of men. I
think that I should feel it hard if I had to be banished from my large
congregation and from my thousands of hearers to a small village
where I could only preach the Gospel to a little company of people. Yet
I am sure that, if I entered fully into the spirit of our Lord's words—
"Not as I will, but as thou wilt"—I should be quite as ready to be there
as to be here. I have heard that among the Jesuits such is the extraordinary obedience which they are compelled to pay to their superiors that,
on one occasion, there was a president of one of their colleges who had
written some of the most learned books in any language—a man of the
highest talents—and the superior of the order took a freak into his head,
for some reason, to send him straight away from the country where he
was to Bath, to stand there in the street for a year and sweep the crossing. And the man did it. He was compelled to do it. His vow obliged
him to do anything that he was told to do.

Now, in a spiritual sense, this is hard to perform. But, nevertheless, it
is a Christian's duty. We remember the saying of a good man that the
angels in heaven are so completely given up to obedience to God that,
if there should be two works to do—ruling an empire and sweeping a
crossing—neither of the two angels who might be selected to go on
these two errands would have any choice in the matter, but would just

leave it with their Lord to decide which part they were to fulfill. You may, perhaps, be called from the charge of the services in a place of worship to become one of the humblest members in another church. You may be taken from a place of much honor and put in the very lowest ranks of the army. Are you willing to submit to that kind of treatment? Your flesh and blood say, "Lord, if I may still serve in Your army, let me be a captain; or, at least, let me be a sergeant or a corporal. If I may help to draw Your chariot, let me be the leading horse, let me run first in the team. Let me wear the showy ribbons." But God may say to you, "I have put you there in the thick of the battle, now I will place you behind. I have given you vigor and strength to fight with great success, now I will make you tarry by the stuff. I have done with you in the prominent position, now I will use you somewhere else." But if we can only pray this prayer, "Not as I will, but as thou wilt," we shall be ready to serve God anywhere and everywhere, so long as we know that we are doing His will.

But there is another trial which we shall all have to endure in our measure, which will prove whether we understand by this prayer what Christ meant by it. Sometimes, *in the service of Christ, we must be prepared to endure the loss of reputation, of honor, and even of character itself.* I remember when I first came to London to preach the Word, I thought that I could bear anything for Christ. But I found myself shamefully slandered, all manner of falsehoods were uttered concerning me. In agony I fell on my face before God and cried to Him. I felt as though that was a thing I could not bear. My character was very dear to me, and I could not endure to have such false things said about me. Then this thought came to me, "You must give up all to Christ. You must surrender everything for Him, character, reputation, and all that you have. If it is the Lord's will, you shall be reckoned the vilest of the vile, so long as you can still continue to serve Him, and your character is really pure, you need not fear. If it is your Master's will that you shall be trampled and spit upon by all the wicked men in the world, you must simply bear it, and say, 'Not as I will, but as thou wilt.'" And I remember then how I rose from my knees and sang to myself that verse—

> If on my face, for thy dear name,
>   Shame and reproaches be,
> All hail reproach, and welcome shame,
>   If thou remember me.

"But how hard it was," you say, "for you to suffer the loss of character and to have evil things spoken against you falsely for Christ's name's sake!" And what was the reason why it was so hard? Why, it was just because I had not fully learned how to pray this prayer of our

Lord Jesus Christ—and I am afraid that I have not completely learned it yet. It is a very delightful thing to have even our enemies speaking well of us, to go through this world with such holiness of character that men who pour scorn upon all religion cannot find fault with us. But it is an equally glorious thing for us to be set in the pillory of shame, to be pelted by every passer-by, to be the song of the drunkard, to be the by-word of the swearer, when we do not deserve it, and to endure all this for Christ's sake. This is true heroism. This is the meaning of the prayer of our text.

Again, some of you have at times thought, "Oh, if the Master will only be pleased to open a door for me where I may be the means of doing good! *How glad I should be if I could have either more wealth, or more influence, or more knowledge, or more talents with which I might serve Him better!*" You have prayed about the matter and thought about it, and you have said, "If I could only get into such-and-such a position, how excellently should I be able to serve God!" You have seen your Master give to some of His servants ten talents, but He has given you only one. You have gone on your knees and asked Him to be good enough to trust you with two, and He has refused it. Or you have had two and you have asked Him to let you have ten; He has said, "No, I will give you two talents, and no more." But you say, "Is it not a laudable desire that I should seek to do more good?" Certainly; trade with your talents, multiply them if you can. But suppose you have no power of utterance, suppose you have no opportunities of serving God, or even suppose the sphere of your influence is limited, what then? Why, you are to say, "Lord, I hoped it was Your will that I might have a wider sphere. But if it is not, although I long to serve You on a larger scale, I will be quite content to glorify You in my present narrower sphere. I feel that here is an opportunity for the trial of my faith and resignation, and again I say, 'Not as I will, but as thou wilt.'"

Christian men, are you prepared heartily to pray this prayer? I fear there is not a single individual among us who could pray it in all its fullness of meaning. Perhaps you may go as far as I have already gone. But if God should take you at your word and say, "My will is that your wife should be smitten with a fatal illness and, like a fading lily, droop and die before your eyes. My will is that your children should be caught up to My loving bosom in heaven and that your house should be burned with fire. My will is that you should be left penniless, a pauper dependent on the charity of others. It is My will that you should cross the sea and that you should go to distant lands and endure unheard-of hardships. It is my will that, at last, your bones should be bleaching on the desert sand in some foreign clime." Are you willing to endure all this for Christ? Remember that you have not attained to the full meaning of this prayer until you have said "Yes" to all that it means. Until you can go to the uttermost lengths to which God's providence may go, you have not gone to the full extent of the resignation in this cry of our Lord.

Many of the early Christians, I think, did know this prayer by heart. It is wonderful how willing they were to do anything and be anything for Christ. They had gotten this idea into their heads that they were not to live to themselves, and they had it also in their hearts. They believed that to be martyred was the highest honor they could possibly wish for. Consequently, if they were brought to the tribunals of the judges, they never ran away from their persecutors. They almost courted death, for they thought it was the highest privilege that they could possibly have if they might be torn in pieces by the lions in the arena or be decapitated with the sword. Now, if we also could but get that idea into our hearts, with what courage would it gird us. How fully might we then serve God, and how patiently might we endure persecution if we had but learned the meaning of this prayer, "Not as I will, but as thou wilt."

Why This Prayer Should Be Our Constant Cry

In the second place, I am to try and give you some reasons why it will be best for us all to seek to have the Holy Spirit within us so that we may be brought into this frame of mind and heart.

And the first reason is, because it is simply *a matter of right*. God ought to have His way at all times, and I ought not to have mine whenever it is contrary to His. If ever my will is at cross purposes to the will of the Supreme, it is but right that mine should yield to His. If I could have my own way—if such a poor, feeble creature as I am could thwart the Omnipotent Creator—it would be wrong for me to do it. What! has He made me, and shall He not do as He wills with me? Is He like the potter, and am I but as the clay, and shall the thing formed say to Him that formed it, "Why have You made me thus?" No, my Lord, it is but right that You should do what You please with me, for I am Yours— Yours, for You have made Me; Yours, for You have bought me with Your blood. If I am a jewel purchased with the precious blood of Jesus then He may cut me into what shape He pleases, He may polish me as He chooses. He may let me be in the darkness of the casket, or let me glitter in His hand or in His diadem. In fact, He may do with me just as He wills, for I am His. So long as I know that He does it, I must say, "Whatever He does is right. My will shall not be in opposition to His will."

But, again, this is not only a matter of right, *it is a matter of wisdom with us*. Depend upon it, dear friends, if we could have our own will, it would often be the worst thing in the world for us. But to let God have

His way with us, even if it were in our power to thwart Him, would be an act of wisdom on our part. What do I desire when I wish to have my own will? I desire my own happiness. Well, but I shall get it far more easily if I let God have His will, for the will of God is both for His own glory and my happiness. So, however much I may think that my own will would tend to my comfort and happiness, I may rest assured that God's will would be infinitely more profitable to me than my own. Although God's will may seem to make it dark and dreary for me at the time, yet from seeming evil He will bring forth good, such as never could have been produced from that supposed good after which my weak and feeble judgment is so apt to run.

But, again, suppose it were possible for us to have our own will, *would it not be an infringement of that loving reliance which Christ may well ask at our hands that we should trust Him?* Are we not saved by trusting our Lord Jesus Christ? Has not faith in Christ been the means of saving me from sin and hell? Then, surely I must not run away from this rule when I come into positions of trial and difficulty. If faith has been superior to sin through the blood of Christ, it will certainly be superior to trial through the almighty arm of Christ. Did I not tell Him when I first came to Him that I would trust no one but Him? Did I not declare that all my other confidences were burst and broken, and scattered to the winds? Did I not ask that He would permit me to put my trust in Him alone? Shall I, after that, play the traitor? Shall I now set up some other object in which to place my trust? Oh, no! my love to Jesus, my gratitude to Him for His condescension in accepting my faith, binds me henceforth to trust to Him, and to Him alone.

We often lose the force of a truth by not making it palpable to our own mind. Let us try to make this one so. Imagine the Lord Jesus to be visibly present in this pulpit. Suppose that He looks down upon one of you, and says, "My child, your will and Mine do not, just now, agree. You desire such-and-such a thing, but I say, 'No, you must not have it.' Now, My child, which will is to prevail, Mine or yours?" Suppose you were to reply, "Lord, I must have my will." Do you not think He would look at you with eyes of infinite sadness and pity, and say to you, "What! did I give up My will for you, and will you not give up your will for Me? Did I surrender all I had, even My life, for your sake, and do you say, you self-willed child, 'I must have these things according to my will, and contrary to Your wish and purpose, O my Savior'?" Surely you could not talk like that. Rather, I think I see you instantly falling on your knees and saying, "Lord Jesus, forgive me forever harboring such evil thoughts. No, my Lord, even if Your will be hard, I will think it pleasant. If it be bitter, I will believe that the bitterest draught is sweet. Let me but see You dying on the cross for me. Let me only know that

You love me. Wherever You shall put me, I will be in heaven as long as I can feel that it is Your will that is being done with me. I will be perfectly content to be just wherever You choose me to be, and to suffer whatever You choose for me to endure." Yes, dear friends, it would show a sad want of that love which we owe to Christ, and of that gratitude which He deserves, if we were once to set our wills up in opposition to His. Therefore, again, beloved, for love's sake, for wisdom's sake, for right's sake, I beseech you ask the Holy Spirit to teach you this prayer of our Lord Jesus Christ and to impart to you its blessed meaning.

The Effect of Truly Saying and Feeling This Prayer

The first effect is *constant happiness*. If you would find out the cause of most of your sorrows, dig at the root of your self-will for that is where it lies. When your heart is wholly sanctified to God and your will is entirely subdued to Him, the bitter becomes sweet, pain is changed to pleasure, and suffering is turned into joy. It is not possible for that man's mind to be disturbed whose will is wholly resigned to the will of God. "Well," says one, "that is a very startling statement." Another says, "I have really sought to have my will resigned to God's will, yet I am disturbed." Yes, and that is simply because though you have sought, like all the rest of us, you have not yet attained to full resignation to the will of the Lord. But when once you have attained to it—I fear you never will in this life—then shall you be free from everything that shall cause you sorrow or discomposure of mind.

Another blessed effect of this prayer, if it is truly presented, is, that *it will give a man holy courage and bravery*. If my mind is wholly resigned to God's will, what have I to fear in all the world? It is with me then as it was with Polycarp. When the Roman emperor threatened that he would banish him, he said, "Thou canst not, for the whole world is my Father's house, and thou canst not banish me from it." "But I will slay thee," said the emperor. "Nay, thou canst not, for my life is hid with Christ in God." "I will take away all thy treasures." "Nay, thou canst not; for I have nothing that thou knowest of; my treasure is in heaven, and my heart is there also." "But I will drive thee away from men, and thou shalt have no friend left." "Nay, that thou canst not do, for I have a Friend in heaven from whom thou canst not separate me; I defy thee, for there is nothing that thou canst do unto me." And so can the Christian always say, if once his will agrees with God's will. He may defy all men, and defy hell itself, for he will be able to say, "Nothing can happen to me that is contrary to the will of God. If it be His will, it is my will, too. If it pleases God, it pleases me. God has been pleased to give me part of His will, so I am satisfied with whatever he sends."

Man is, after all, only the second cause of our sorrows. A persecutor says, perhaps, to a child of God, "I can afflict you." "No, you cannot, for you are dependent on the first Great Cause, and He and I are agreed." Ah! dear friends, there is nothing that makes men such cowards as having wills contrary to the will of God. But when we resign ourselves wholly into the hands of God, what have we to fear? The thing that made Jacob a coward was that he was not resigned to God's will when Esau came to meet him. God had foretold that the elder of the two sons of Isaac should serve the younger. Jacob's business was to believe that and to go boldly forward with his wives and children. He was not to bow down before Esau, but to say, "The promise is, 'The elder shall serve the younger' (Gen. 25:23; Rom. 9:12). I am not going to bow down to you. It is your place to fall prostrate before me." But poor Jacob said, "Perhaps it is God's will that Esau should conquer me, and smite the mothers and their children; but my will is that it shall not be so." The contest is well pictured at the ford Jabbok. But if Jacob had not disbelieved God's promise, he would never have bowed himself to the earth seven times before his brother Esau. In the holy majesty of his faith he would have said, "Esau, my brother, you can do me no harm, for you can do nothing contrary to the will of God. You can do nothing contrary to His decree, and I will be pleased with whatsoever it is."

So, this resignation to God's will gives, first, joy in the heart, then it gives fearless courage, and yet another thing follows from it. As soon as anyone truly says, "Not as I will, but as thou wilt," this resolve *tends to make every duty light, every trial easy, every tribulation sweet.* We should never feel it to be a hard thing to serve God. Yet there are many people, who, if they do a little thing for the Lord, think so much of it. If there is ever a great thing to be done, you have, first, to plead very hard to get them to do it. When they do it, very often it is done so badly that you are half sorry you ever asked them to do it. A great many people make very much out of what is really very little. They take one good action which they have performed and hammer it out until it becomes as thin as gold leaf, and then they think they may cover a whole week with that one good deed. The seven days shall all be glorified by an action which only takes five minutes to perform. It shall be quite enough, they even think, for all time to come. But the Christian, whose will is conformed to God's will, says, "My Lord, is there anything else for me to do? Then, I will gladly do it. Does it involve want of rest? I will do it. Does it involve loss of time in my business? Does it involve me, sometimes, in toil and fatigue? Lord, it shall be done if it is Your will, for Your will and mine are in complete agreement. If it is possible, I will do it. I will count all things but loss that I may win Christ and be found in him, rejoicing in His righteousness and not in mine own."

The Only Way to Obtain This Prayer
Is through the Holy Spirit

There are many other sweet and blessed effects which this resignation would produce. But I must close by observing that the only way in which this spirit can be attained is by the unction of the Holy One, the outpouring and the indwelling of the Holy Spirit in our hearts.

You may try to subdue your own self, but you will never do it alone. You may labor, by self-denial, to keep down your ambition, but you will find that it takes another shape and grows by that wherewith you thought to poison it. You may seek to concentrate all the love of your soul on Christ, and in the very act you will find self creeping in. I am sometimes astonished—and yet not astonished when I know the evil of my own heart—when I look within myself and find how impure my motive is at the very moment when I thought it was most pure. I expect it is the same with you, dear friends. You perform a good action—some almsgiving to the poor, perhaps. You say, "I will do it very quietly." Someone speaks of it, and you say at once, "I wish you had not spoken of that. I do not like to hear anyone talk of what I have done. It hurts me." Perhaps it is only your pride that makes you say that it hurts you, for some folk make their modesty to be their pride. It is, in fact, their secret pride that they are doing good, and that people do not know it. They glory in that supposed secrecy, and by its coming out they feel that their modesty is spoiled. They are afraid that people will say, "Ah, you see that it is known what they do. They do not really do their good deeds in secret." So that even our modesty may be our pride. What some people think their pride may happen to be the will of God, and may be real modesty. It is very hard work to give up our own will. But it is possible, and that is one of the lessons we should learn from this text, "Not as I will, but as thou wilt."

Again, if there is anybody of whom you are a little envious— perhaps a minister who takes a little of the gloss off you by preaching better than you do, or a Sunday school teacher who is more successful in his work—make that particular person the object of your most constant prayer, and endeavor as much as lies in you to increase that person's popularity and success. Someone asks, "But you cannot bring human nature up to that point, can you—to try and exalt one's own rival?" My dear friends, you will never know the full meaning of this prayer until you have tried to do this and actually sought to honor your rival more than yourself. That is the true spirit of the Gospel, "in honour preferring one another" (Rom. 12:10). I have sometimes found it hard work, I must confess. But I have schooled myself down to it. Can this be done? Yes, John the Baptist did it. He said of Jesus, "He must increase, but I must decrease" (John 3:30). If you had asked John whether he wished to increase, he would have said, "Well, I should like to have more disciples. Still, if it is the Lord's will, I am quite content to go down and that Christ should go up."

How important, therefore, it is for us to learn how we may attain to this state of acquiescence with our heavenly Father's will! I have given you the reasons for it, but how can it be done? Only by the operation of the Spirit of God. As for flesh and blood, they will not help you in the least, they will go just the other way. When you think that, surely, you have gotten flesh and blood under control, you will find that they have gotten the upper hand of you just when you thought you were conquering them. Pray the Holy Spirit to abide with you, to dwell in you, to baptize you, to immerse you in His sacred influence, to cover you, to bury you in His sublime power. So, and only so, when you are completely immersed in the Spirit and steeped, as it were, in the crimson sea of the Savior's blood, shall you be made fully to realize the meaning of this great prayer, "Not as I will, but as thou wilt." "Lord, not self, but Christ; not my own glory, but Your glory; not my aggrandizement, but Yours. No, not even my success, but Your success; not the prosperity of my own church or my own self, but the prosperity of Your church, the increase of Your glory—let all that be done as You will, not as I will."

How different this is from everything connected with the world! I have tried to take you up to a very high elevation. If you have been able to get up there, or even to pant to get up there, how striking has the contrast been between this spirit and the spirit of the worldling! I shall not say anything to those of you who are unconverted, except this: Learn how contrary you are to what God would have you be, and what you must be, before you can enter the kingdom of heaven. You know that you could not say, "Let God have His will." You know also that you could not humble yourself to become as a little child. This shows your deep depravity. So, may the Holy Spirit renew you, for you have need of renewing that you may be made a new creature in Christ Jesus! May He sanctify you wholly, spirit, soul, and body, and at last present you, faultless, before the throne of God, for His dear name's sake! Amen.